CUAY

S. Denise King

I0081543

C U A Y

/'KWAY'/

CLEAN UP AFTER YOURSELF

Matthew 6:33

Seek first the kingdom and his righteousness and all other things will be added unto you.

CUAY   *S. Denise King*

CUAY.org
@CUAYlife

Designed by Sadiya Kiburi

ISBN   (9780602072490)

For information on bulk purchases, please contact The Gratitude Group PR at 754-900-7429 or write **info@prgratitude.org**

First edition update: May 19, 2021

10 9 8 7 6 5 4 3 2 1

C U A Y ©

◀◀◀ ◀ /'KWAY'/

CLEAN UP AFTER YOURSELF

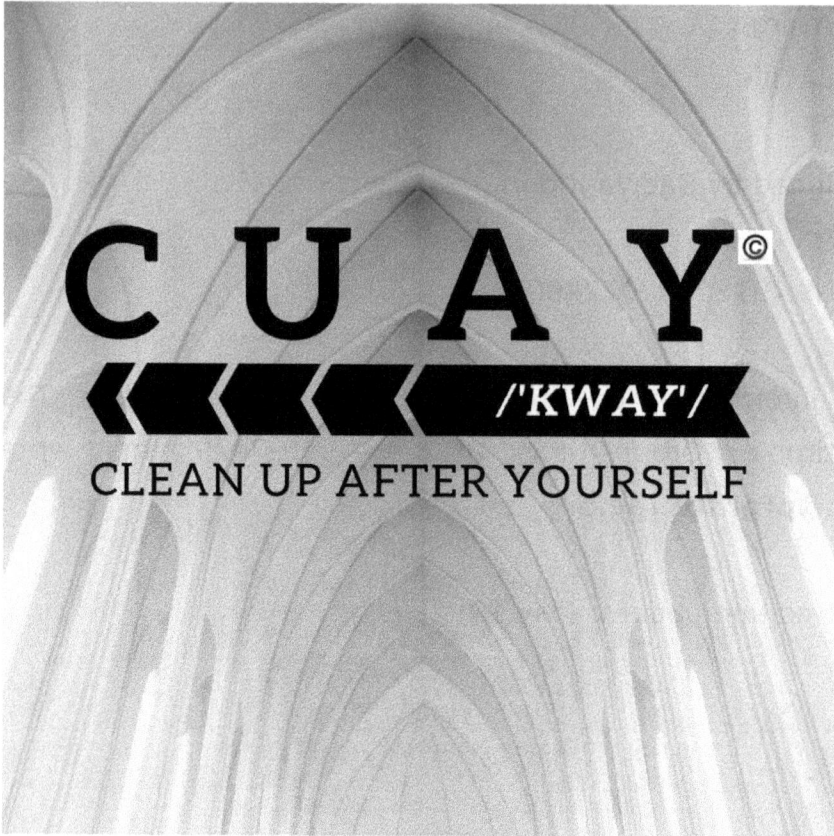

To the seekers who wander without guidance, those uncomfortable asking and those who never knew what to ask. You were heard.

To those who taught me to maintain order in my life...I honor you and my children's children with this gift. Slowly, quickly and thoroughly.

VOCAB ALERT

Become familiar with some new terminology.

CUAY /'kway'/ : *verb*
clean up after yourself

CUAYing /'kway-ing'/ : *verb*
cleaning up after yourself

CUAYer /'kway-er'/ : *noun*
a person that cleans up after his or herself

CUAYville /'kway-vil'/ : *noun*
the mental space/mindset of learning how to clean up after oneself

CUAYologist /'kway-ol-uh-jist'/ : *noun*
a person who has mastered how to clean up after his or herself

CUAYed /'kway-d'/ : *verb*
the past tense of cleaning up after yourself. It is done.

See glossary for other terms noted in the text with *

TABLE OF CONTENTS

Introduction to Cuaying

While attempting to maintain some form of sanity, many families have become unbalanced when it comes to cleaning up after themselves. Through the process of growing up, raising a family, and getting used to working 40 plus hours a week to provide for that family, you will quickly realize organization is essential. Any stress and disharmony at home will impact your entire life, your goals, ambitions, and intentions. This text is written to help bridge the gap between what you know is necessary to lead a happy and healthy life and your actual reality. When you begin to fully appreciate the life you are giving, you move through it with care and concern, mindful of the trail you leave behind. The process of CUAYing (cleaning up after yourself) means taking responsibility for your own being and recognizing how personal accountability affects your life, the lives of those around you, and essentially the world.

This book is an interpretation of the lifestyles I've studied from my birth mother, godmothers, grandmothers, aunts, uncles, sisters, big brother, and friends throughout the years. Seeing disorder impact families negatively has been difficult, especially knowing that all they needed was a talk with grandma, a lesson from a sister, or that tip from auntie. But what happens when no one taught you how to properly clean up after yourself? What happens when you still wipe yourself wrong as an adult? What kind of adult will you be when you have a mother who never allowed you to CUAY? Or when you can't afford a maid this year? How will generations that don't CUAY affect the planet?

As you journey through the chapters of this book it is important to keep in mind that this is a guide to help establish order in your dome and home. It is not a quick fix, cookie-cutter solution to your issue. It will take conscious effort and intention from all essential parties or simply your whole self for CUAY to work for you. CUAY will look different for each individual and family, but the concept remains the same. This text is written for you to teach yourself to CUAY, but it's even better to have your family read it together. Parents will be relieved to find a fun solution to gently encourage their children to gain accountability for what they leave behind, and make CUAYing all day a lifestyle instead of a constant family worry. If you are tired of repeating "Clean up after yourself," knowing that your loved one either doesn't seem to follow through or doesn't know what cleaning up after his or herself looks like, allow this guide to support your efforts.

Ultimately, the goal should be to find the CUAY that returns you and/or your family back into balance. The order that helps you all stay centered on your goals. The accountability that CUAYing is no longer a second thought, but truly a way of living. To clean up after yourself automatically is to recognize that you are responsible for your impact on your home and personal hygiene first and foremost. Everyone plays a role, not only in your homes, but in your communities, our nation, and our world. Cuaying is not just an American problem- it is a global necessity. Take a look around the room you are sitting in right now. Stroll through your local neighborhoods or go on virtual field trips around your global community. You will likely see the impact disorder has on many different environments. Disorder affects our domes (minds) as well as our homes and personal interactions with others. Now we have a solution that is ready to stand the test of time: CUAY!

This is a revolutionary self-empowerment mission that can start as young as seven years old. Yes, seven. By then, children are generally reading and learning to comprehend on a deeper level. For young readers, you may need adult interpretation to process some of the content here. Ask someone to help you if you don't understand. Or better yet, ask the author personally, me. Tag the book on social media, @CUAYlife. By the time readers reach the age of 15 you should be CUAYing independently and able to deep clean an entire home. No worries if your teenage years are far behind you. Give yourself a timeline to move through these lessons and become a CUAY professional at any stage of life.

CUAY changed everything for us. It is a methodology that helped our family of various cleaning mentalities get along and lead a happier home life together. It ended up making room for our lives to expand and having a clean home opened doors for other creative ideas to come alive. We immediately recognized the need to spread this method outside of the walls of our home to other families and individuals who could benefit from it. We began to tell others about it, but it is more than one conversation. CUAY is a lifestyle. So, we had to write it out.

CUAY came easily to me as an idea, but I had to explain it to my children and others along the way. My task was then to break it down and demonstrate its value. This book is written to do just that. We hope you learn something new and pass on the message in your home, classroom, or community. It's not just about delegation and telling growing children or loved ones what CUAYing is. It is empowering yourself and your family to crave a clean temple, environment, and world.

It's time. You are about to enter CuayVille. You'll learn a collection of useful new words, read interesting stories and get personal when it comes to getting your dome and home right. This is not a place for bashfulness or any kind of embarrassment. It is a place of authenticity and growth. For those who are pretty clean already, here is your opportunity to put it into words, so you can teach others how to CUAY. For those who need support mastering CUAYing, tune all the way in. You might be surprised how easy it can be.

Immerse yourself into the words on the pages to follow and place them deep in your mind. Study CUAY step by step. It is written with the intention of comprehension beyond what you read, but for you to maneuver through life differently after digesting it fully. Are you ready to dive in?

Remember, it takes a village to grow into a fully functioning adult. So, don't be ashamed if you encounter areas here that no one ever told you needed attention. There are so many areas that can be overlooked for parents and guardians to teach youth in their care. CUAYing is our new standard. It is also recognized that some children have no guidance at all, just older people that feed them. In an attempt to serve the whole village in the areas of keeping their domes and homes in order, CUAYing was born.

Now is the time for you to walk through the steps, master the CUAY way and share it far and wide with anyone you think could benefit from it. Enjoy the freedom it brings.

Regards,

S. Denise King, MPA

CHAPTER ONE

WHAT IS CUAYING?

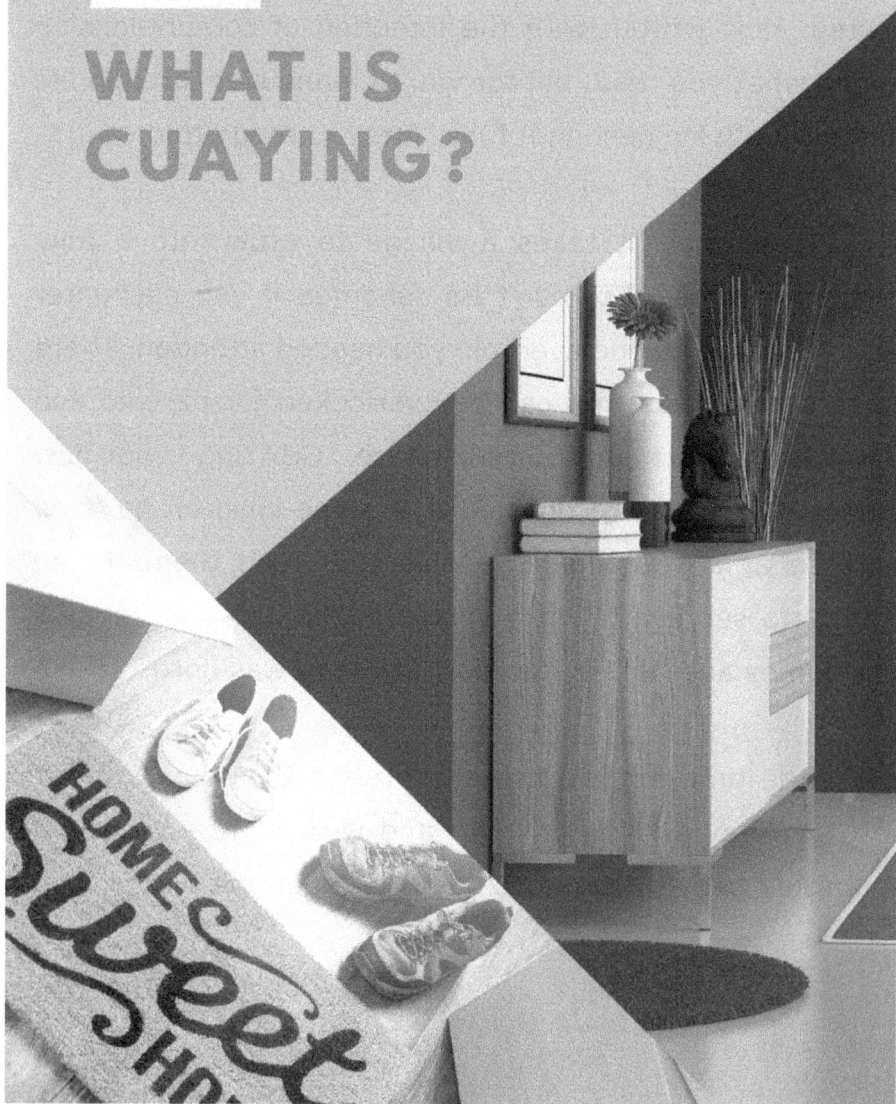

Chapter 1
What is Cuaying?

At the moment we are born into our human vessels, we are totally dependent on someone else. Someone to feed, bathe, clothe, shelter, and love us. Each one of us requires someone to pay attention to our needs and meet them. In order to survive that year from birth to toddlerhood, we have to overcome the primary task of surrendering control to someone else. Our caregivers have to do everything for us, down to our most private care. They keep our butts clean. It's a labor of love and one that some may want to forget. For people who are super independent, thinking of depending on someone to even get them a glass of water is unmentionable, let alone someone to keep them alive.

These folks are so accustomed to doing it all for themselves. For many- cleaning is innate- it's natural. Some may even say it's automatic. But what about the other side of the coin? There are those who wholeheartedly enjoy others doing for them. They start off in those toddlers and never mastered how to click that automatic clean button within themselves. It's not that they want to live in a mess, but they put off getting to the mess until a later time and before you know it, they look up to a HOT mess. It seems that they get used to being taken care of during those formative years on earth (infancy) and grow to expect it as their norm throughout their lifetime. The moment I saw this happening in my family I knew that I had to shut it down before it settled into a character trait. This is how the CUAY mantra began.

Basically, in order to be a functional citizen of the world, babies have to develop autonomy. There is a shift when the dependency on others is now transferred to the individual. Different families, tribes, and cultures allow this transition time to happen at various points in life. Some start around preschool ages at three or four years old, asking children to put away toys after playtime. Others wait until kindergarten and grade school to have children clean up after themselves. My mother taught us to require children to clean up the same day they start walking. It's like a rites of passage. For most, that would mean CUAY begins between 10-13 months. Yes, months. I communicated this to both of my children early on during the first year of life. They start by walking their dirty diapers to the trash or cleaning up food and of course, their toys. At this age children still see cleaning as a game.

Somehow, between the four years of raising my daughter and the arrival of my son, I forgot that I had to reteach these lessons. My son was beginning to let life pile up around him. Although he knew how to put things back, he had no motivation to do it. Other things continuously took precedence over CUAYing. At this point, he didn't know what CUAYing was. He was missing my example of how to deep clean our home and environment, coupled with his growing screen time addiction. Instead, all-day every day, I could see his mark left all over the place from his belongings. With two children, ages 9 and 13 at the time, and each of us with bags and belongings to tend to, maintaining a tidy space was becoming a major problem at home.

My son would complete most tasks extremely quickly, but often inadequately. He'd sweep the floor but leave the dust pile, take the trash out but not replace the bag or leave trash in the can beneath the new bag. When he came home from school, he would leave a trail of everything he did from the moment he came in the door. Shoes were left by the door, a hoodie thrown on the floor and the light left on in the bathroom. Cereal box left open on the counter, and crumbs from a snack still on the table along with all of his book bag content. All this in less than an hour. And just imagine the mess after his evening bath. It was difficult and I felt like I was nagging him about cleaning far too often. Repeating myself about tidiness took over our family time- when all I wanted was to enjoy our time at home together.

My daughter, on the other hand, was usually meticulous. She moved with intention and seemed to be calculated in how and why she would leave something behind. Leaving things behind was less likely for her because she knew that would mean someone else would be messing with it. Or that it might get "lost in the sauce" as we liked to say. Most often, if she left something behind... It was to leave a message or send a clue. Like a Krispy Kreme coupon found on my favorite seat. Or a flyer for a friend's weekend party left on my bed after our family prayer at night.

She was different. Cuaying was easy for her. It was natural for her to take time and pay attention to all the details that surrounded her. It was amazing to watch CUAY come alive for my oldest child because it was the first time I transferred all the tips from my elders and taught her what a standard of living looked like in action. She begged us to allow her to pick out her own clothes and get dressed from the age of two. By the time she was four, she asked if she could move out from home and live with a friend.

"FOUR AND READY TO MOVE OUT"

"Time to take your bath, Zenobia. You had a full day at the birthday party. Time to shut it down for the night."

"Yes, ma'am." Grabbing her housecoat and towel, she moved to the bathroom to her already running bathwater.

I noticed that the water stopped, but didn't hear her get in, even after 5 minutes in the bathroom alone. I rushed to the bathroom with my 8-month-old son on my hip and opened the door to a puzzled 4-year-old sitting on the closed toilet seat in deep thought.

"Zenobia, what are you doing? Are you okay?"

"Yes, mommy," she said casually before looking up and responding, "Would you be mad if I moved out?"

"Excuse me?"

"I mean, I would still see you sometimes but... I was thinking I could live with Mama Amber instead."

Huh... I thought, wondering where in the world the idea had come from.

"I like it over there," she continued.

I was bewildered. My 4-year-old just asked me to move out of the house.

Frozen in the hallway holding a wiggling, half-naked baby Saadiq, I wondered who else had a preschooler that wanted to move out that I could conference with regarding this blow to my ego.

Quickly realizing I was in uncharted territory, I demanded, "Girl, get in the bathtub and get ready for bed," using my sternness to mask the fact that I had no clue how to maneuver this scenario. Rushing to the master bedroom to call their daddy for help, I held on to the clinging baby in a football hold under my arm. For him, it was an adventure.

Saadiq laughed as I hastily dialed not to let the panic seep in.

"Please hurry home," I pleaded when my then-husband picked up the phone. "She said she wants to move out."

"Who?" He responded, not considering it was his darling "babygirl".

"Zenobia," I blurted out. He laughed for a moment, but my silence communicated the seriousness.

"Really? Why?"

"I guess she doesn't want to be a part of this family anymore."

"Does she want to get her own place or what?" He responded, partly in sarcasm while also probing the magnitude of the situation.

"No, she wants to live with Amber".

"I'm almost there. I'll talk to her when I get home."

I guess he didn't know what to say either. Amber was a community mom who we'd been spending time with over the past few months. Her youngest baby was the same age as Saadiq, and she had a daughter that Zenobia was fond of. They were growing up as sisters.

I dreaded the follow-up questions that I was certain would continue after her bath. I hoovered by the bathroom door, hoping their daddy would arrive before she left the bathroom. When I heard the water begin to drain out of the tub, I started to pace the floor. Unsure of how much time I had until she'd be back to her pre-bath thoughts.

Pacing the hallway and peeping through the bathroom door, I watched as she ensured the bar of soap didn't slide into the tub. She grabbed the low odor bath cleaner and read aloud, "Low odor, clean and fresh," and sprayed the tub carefully.

Still mindful not to breathe any of those "low odor" fumes, she turned around and hit the switch to turn on the exhaust fan. I ducked back a bit to conceal my peeking. She located the scrubbing brush and brought the water to a slight trickle, just enough so that the spray didn't quickly wash away. Zenobia started on one side of the tub and I watched her balance on her stomach, exhibiting amazing core strength, she scrubbed the tub all the way around. She turned the water on high and rinsed it. She closed the shower curtain, dried her hands, and proceeded to moisturize. Laying her towel on the floor she slowly opened the whipped shea butter. Struggling a bit, but not giving up, she got it opened and took her time to moisturize her entire four-year-old body. I was so amazed at her careful movement that I didn't notice how much she was applying.

I heard the garage door open and was relieved that I wouldn't have to face this conversation alone. All the pacing and peeping had tired out my playful toddler, who was now heavily asleep in my arms. I laid him down in his room and rushed to meet their daddy downstairs for a debrief before we spoke to Zenobia about the question at hand. Running down the steps and turning the corner he could feel my anxiety.

"Peace," he said. "You talked to her?"
"No, she's almost done in the bathroom though." By the time we reached the top of the stairs, we could see she had finished brushing her teeth, hung her damp towel to dry, and was gathering her dirty clothes before she turned off the bathroom light. We waited in the shadows, watching her walk to her room in her tightly tied pink unicorn housecoat. Dropping her clothes in her hamper she hollered out,

"Mommy!"

"Yes?" I replied as if we were down the hall to camouflage my stalking.

Startled by our proximity, she turned toward us, equally startled by her full-body soul glow from her overly moisturized skin. There was a thick layer over all her visible skin.

"Baby girl, come here," he said as she approached, continuing our pre-bath conversation. Her daddy assisted her with rubbing in the visibly thick layer of shea butter coating her skin and wiping off the excess.

The first thing she said was, "I'm going to need some more skirts."

"Why?" her father and I inquired in unison.

"Because Mama Amber's girls have to wear skirts all the time." She was determined. Her bath brought her to deeper thoughts regarding her decision. I thought she was just taking a bath, but she was busy planning out her next move. She was four.

Carefully, I witnessed her in discussion with her father. She weighed the options and even vowed to be vegan and start wearing long skirts like her friend's family. I was crying on the inside but allowed him to facilitate the conversation. It appeared that her mind was made up. We called Amber to see if we could just play it out. She agreed. The next morning Zenobia was packed and ready. I was mad, #BIGmad. But more hurt that she was so determined to move out.

After two days of living at Mama Amber's house, she was home with a fever and stories of how quickly a new bar of soap disappeared between the family of 6. In a way, she knew how to take care of herself in ways that some adults didn't.

Maybe her level of maturity made her think she was ready to move out. And maybe that's why some parents like to withhold independence from their children as a means to keep them dependent. Were we wrong for teaching her the habit of cleaning up after herself early? Is there a middle ground? Or should we strive to have all our children to master CUAYing before they start elementary school?

Respectfully, I believe that incorporating CUAYing as a necessity for preschoolers will bring about a cleaning world starting from the classroom and beyond.

My daughter is one type of human. The type that prefers order and cleanliness. For her, the act of CUAYing comes easily. However, as previously mentioned, there is another type as well. The other type has varying degrees but ultimately, they are more concerned with their own thoughts, making their surroundings secondary to them. My children were two different breeds and somehow, we had to coexist... peacefully.

Now that you know what CUAYing is and where it originated, let's get busy learning how to CUAY.

You're

Cute

But do you

CUAY

CUAY

24/7

◄◄◄ /'KWAY'/ ►►►

Clean Up After Yourself

CHAPTER TWO

HOW TO CLEAN UP AFTER YOURSELF

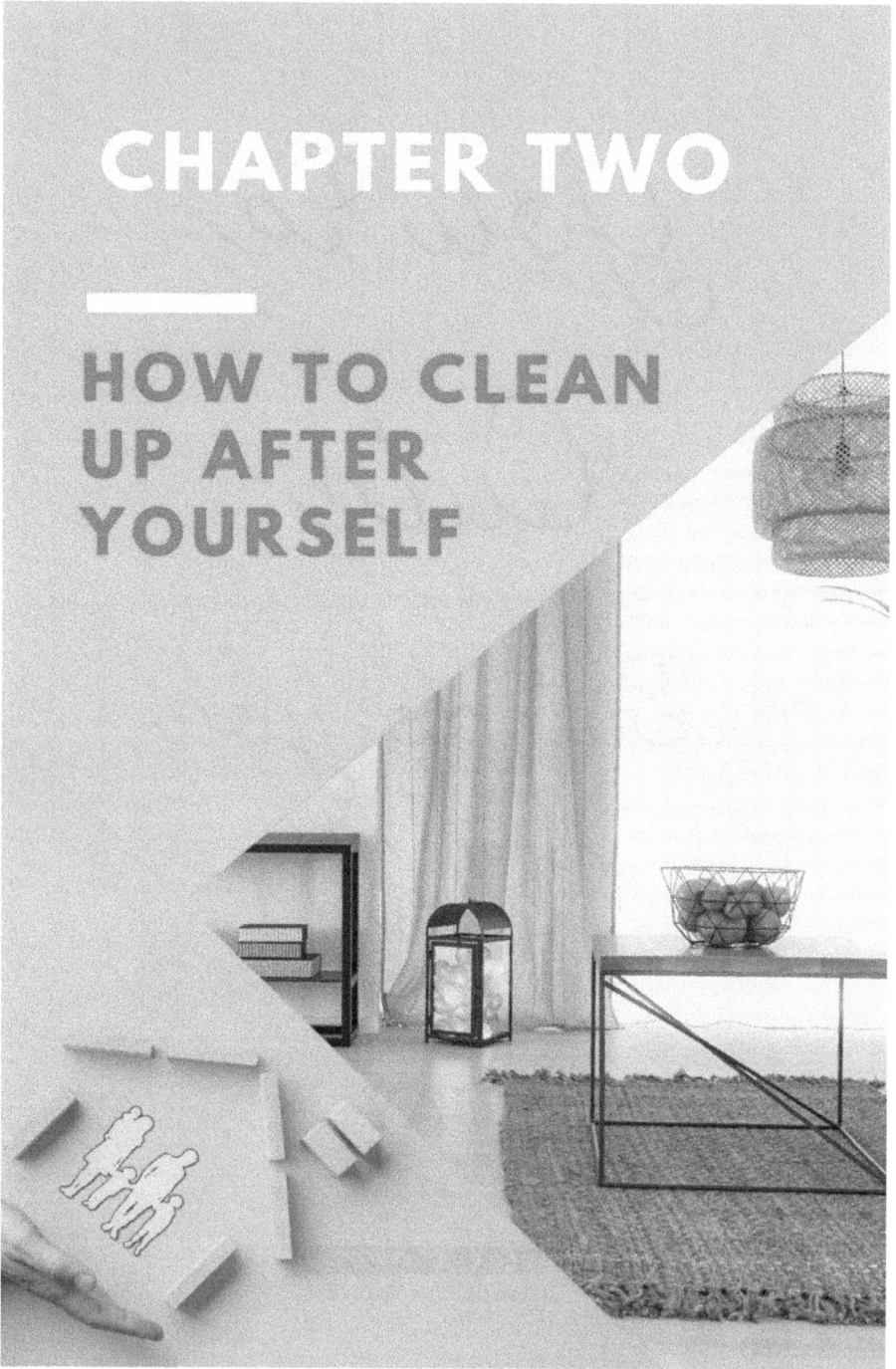

Chapter 2
How to Clean Up After Yourself?

CUAYing became essential when my children shared rooms. They were seven and eleven at the time that we minimized our lifestyle from a two-storied, three-bedroom, two and a half bath home with a garage in North Carolina, to a two-bedroom, two-bathroom apartment in South Florida. The goal was to save to buy a home of our own, so it was a compromise for everyone. I gave the owner's suite to the children to grant more space for their things. For me, this meant a smaller bedroom to house my queen-sized bed and no walk-in closet for my eclectic, urban and corporate-ish wardrobe. Over the two years in our small South Florida apartment, I threatened them many times to switch rooms, hoping it would motivate them to appreciate the space they had more. The threats never worked so instead, I simply outlined how to CUAY step-by-step.

So many families suffer in disorder, not because they don't want to do better, but because they wake up each day unsure of how to make it happen. By applying these steps to your lifestyle, you will find the accountability for CUAY is shifted and shared among the whole family equally. Equally doesn't mean everyone does everything, because some family members may still be learning to become a CUAY professional. Equally meaning, everyone is responsible for the mess, clutter, and trash that they contribute to the environment.

The following is the foundation of Cleaning Up After Yourself. By using these four steps, you will be able to evaluate and CUAY your way through your environment and teach others how to support your efforts. As with most journeys in life, the hardest part is getting started; taking action in the right direction instead of being stuck in a depressing environment that sucks the life out of you.

There are three steps to begin your CUAY journey. These steps can't be skipped or overlooked if your goal is to master the process and become a CUAY professional and they must be repeated to keep CUAYing alive. But be encouraged, it will be worth it and eventually will become thoughtless, you'll just move knowing exactly what needs to be done.

As humans, we live and accumulate things daily. Like mosquitoes to the flesh, it seems we just have to have more *stuff*. Whatever that it is for you or your loved ones, the accumulating leads to clutter and clutter often leads to disorder, physically, and mentally. We buy new things even if we don't really need them. And even when we don't, our skin sheds and our homes get dusty without us moving a muscle. Dirt is bound to accumulate.

Use the following THREE STEPS to activate your CUAY lifestyle. Keep them in mind or set a weekly, monthly, or quarterly timeline to revisit these areas to maintain order in your dome and home.

STEP ONE

SORT & SHARE

Keep
Sell
Donate
Trash

S. DENISE KING

1. <u>STEP ONE: Sort and Share</u>

This was a hard step for me because I am a bag lady at heart. #CueBadu I'm not too proud to gather friends' old clothes and I can find an elegant outfit from a consignment shop without skipping a beat. So, letting go of my beloved shirts and jeans, not to mention shoes and household items was a task to obey. Still, unless I wanted to have baggage bursting from every corner and crevice, I had to downsize. Not just our living space, but the things that filled it to the brim as well. To sort and share you have to begin by sorting out what you have:

- Keep
- Sell
- Donate
- Trash

Keep the things that haven't accumulated dust over the last month or so and sell anything else that may still have a monetary value. There are seasonal items that may have been put away for a time, but you know what gets used and what just takes up space. If need be, have someone help you Sort and Share. This way they can hold you accountable for keeping the "keep" pile as low as possible.

The selling part can be a little tricky because we get so attached to things that sometimes we feel that the value is more than it's worth. I won't specifically name the apps since they haven't endorsed this project, but there are plenty of online marketplace options that you can use to sell your gently used items. Find one or all and post with fair prices. Keep your sale pile in a box or a certain area in the house that is out of the normal flow of traffic.

The Donate pile is the most rewarding. The joy on someone's face when they really appreciate things that you are giving away is quite rewarding. My mother taught us not to give away something that isn't worthy. Some things are just TRASH.

The last step of the Sort and Share when it comes to CUAYing is the trash. If it's broken beyond repair, ripped and worn thin, rusted, or plain gross: just say goodbye to it. If it has sentimental value and you want to have a mini funeral for your beloved item, do that! But take a picture and afterward, LET. IT. GO.

After you Sort and Share you will be surprised how much clearer your space is. But you still have that "keep" pile that needs to be handled.

List Your Sell Worthy Items

_____

_____

_____

_____

_____

_____

_____

_____

> "Many men will not begin an undertaking unless they feel sure they will succeed in it. What a mistake! ... Tackle everything with a feeling that you will utilize all the power within you to make it a success."
>
> Theron Q. Dumont, The Power of Concentration

2 STEP TWO

DEEP CLEAN

Take before and after pictures

Uncover areas usually overlooked

Check and clear all nooks, crannies, crevises and corners

S. DENISE KING

2.   STEP TWO: DEEP CLEAN

I know you're excited to get to work on your environment but there's a step before CUAYing that I didn't mention yet. The Deep Clean. Stop where you are and take a few pictures around your home. These pictures will be important later as you compare your progress and motivate yourself and your family not to let it get too far out of order again.

The Deep Clean is Step 2 because you have to Sort and Share your belongings before you can even see what requires a deep clean. After the clutter is clear you can see what you are working with. So, what is a "Deep Clean"? A Deep Clean is cleaning those areas that are usually overlooked. Under the couch cushions, behind the desk, bookshelf, and appliances in the kitchen. Deep in the bathroom's nooks and crannies.

I know, I know. It's gross in some of those areas. So, if it's too much for you, hire someone to do it. That can be a housekeeping company or a teenager within reach. But if needed, be ready to put a couple of dollars on the line and invest in starting your CUAY experience with a clean slate. This means your environment should be clean to start with.

Take pictures so that everyone knows what it's supposed to look like when the sun comes up in the morning and before the lights go off before bed. If it doesn't look picture-ready or what I like to call "Hotel worthy" then you shouldn't be going to bed yet. A good time to deep clean is when you have the day free. It may take a few hours depending on the size of your home, classroom, office, or car.

Please note: If deep cleaning seems overwhelming to you, odds are your space REALLY needs it. You know what they say: if there's a will, there's away. So, don't give up! Challenge a friend, family, or loved one to start CUAYing and offer to deep clean each other's places as a team. Yes, it might be a bit embarrassing to have all your dirt showing, but at least you won't be doing it alone. Chapter three will clear up your questions on how to deep clean, stay tuned.

List Areas That Need Deep Cleaning

_____

_____

_____

_____

_____

_____

_____

_____

_____

> *"Our homes are like a baby, nurture it daily."*
> *Dr. Ama Bey, Charlotte, NC*

STEP THREE

3

CUAY ALL-DAY

"Be Quick Slow & Thorough."

Quickly remove any signs of you around the room

Slowly scan the scene to clear all clutter and debris

Thoroughly discard and store all items where they belong

S. DENISE KING

3.   <u>STEP THREE: CUAY ALL DAY</u>

You've organized and deep cleaned your area. Now all the things that you found worthy of keeping need a home. If you can't find a home for an item, you need to remove it from the "keep" pile and sell or donate it instead. Immediately! No exceptions. It must have a home of its own. This means nothing else lives in that exact place. Every shelf should be categorized and organized for specific belongings.

CUAYing can actually be done in 15 minutes or less in most rooms. Since everything has a place, it just depends on how long it takes you to move things from where they are, to where they belong. Once you get the hang of it your CUAY time per room will shrink. Whatever your CUAY time is, be sure to add it to your morning and nightly ritual so that things are in order before you leave home and before you go to bed at night. For siblings, this is a great opportunity for a friendly competition. Give them a time frame and reward whoever thoroughly finishes cleaning their room the fastest. After a while, they'll be CUAYing so fast that everyone is rewarded. And if you're the one CUAYing, reward yourself. In the end, the ultimate reward is having a clean home to live in so it's a win-win.

CUAYing is a master chore, but it is also a human responsibility to master cleaning up after yourself at some point in your development. Make tidiness a priority and eventually, it will become a lifestyle for yourself and your household, where everyone is always working towards that goal. This also includes holding each other and ourselves accountable for the messes we contribute.

I know it sounds a little exhausting. But once you get started after Sorting and Sharing, Deep Cleaning, and making sure everything has a home- you realize you're just being a taxi for things to get back where they belong. From then on the secret to CUAYing is to do it all the time. Yes, that means when you finish using that bowl you need to wash it or make sure it makes it to the washing location. And yes, it means that when you leave work for the day you need to CUAY your desk before you walk out.

Set at least two times to CUAY every day that works best for you and your family. I recommend 7 am and 11 pm. Some people are not up by 7 am or already sleep by 11 pm. Or maybe your already out of the house by that time in the morning or not back home at 11 pm. Whatever times you choose set timers on your phones and make it a habit to take at least 15 minutes to check the scene. Taxi those things back where they live. Sweep, vacuum, wipe, trash it, or share it out to someone else that can use it. That's it.

After a while, the daily CUAYing needs are not enough and you have to set aside some time for that deep cleaning again.

In the next chapter, we will take time to go through the house with you and uncover areas that typically need deep cleaning, and offer some ways to get it done. Take a note of the 3 steps as you will be using these steps on-going along your CUAYing journey.

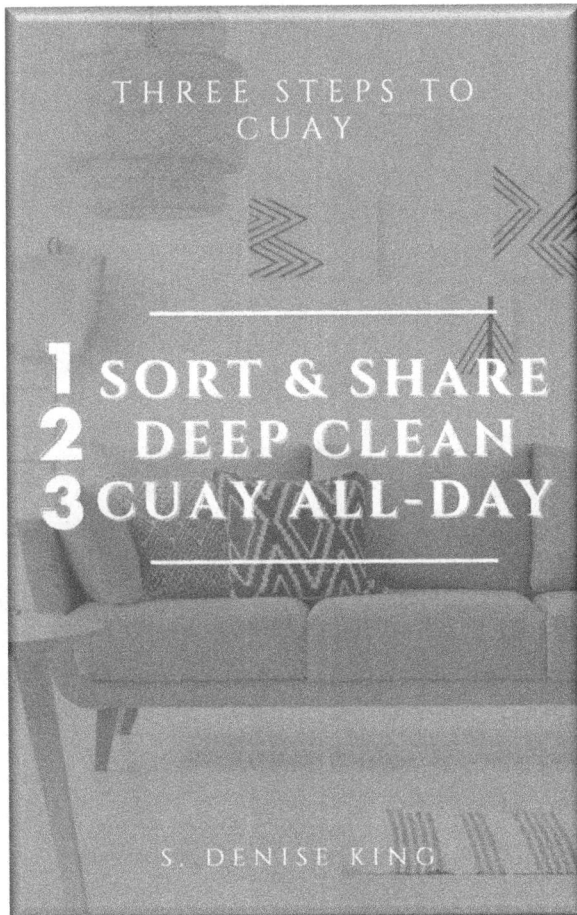

THREE STEPS TO CUAY

1 SORT & SHARE
2 DEEP CLEAN
3 CUAY ALL-DAY

S. DENISE KING

CHAPTER THREE

___

THE DEEP CLEANING GUIDE

Chapter 3
The Deep Cleaning Guide

Setting the stage to CUAY

There is a mood for cleaning. If you don't carry it with you, you have to create it. It should be cheerful and intentional. This means you consciously move through your home or space, thinking with the end in mind. Yes, think CLEAN! So, before you begin to deep clean, get your mind right. Start your favorite playlist of music, gospel, electronica, jazz, hip-hop, oldies, underground, or whatever puts you in a good place. Open the windows if possible, for airflow, raise the blinds to let some extra light in. BREATHE... but not too deep just in case it's still dusty around there.:)

If you're looking around right now thinking there's no hope for your home. More than likely it just needs deep cleaning for you to activate its potential. Did you know there is a sacred flow to cleaning, where you gracefully move from room to room? Raising the vibration with eco-friendly cleaning supplies or old-fashioned bleach, soap, and water. Ridding every inch from debris, clutter, or trash. But don't worry, I won't be pressuring you here to clean that particular way. You have options. There's also the "any means necessary" hurricane cleaning technique that works just the same. The goal doesn't change but the in-between may look a little different.

My style of cleaning usually looks like chaos because I use the hurricane cleaning technique. I move from room to room, mixing tasks and making cleaning decisions until chaos blurs into cleaned! It works and there is no one way to get to the goal. Just keep moving and hold the vision. Think CLEAN!

In an effort to guide you through the DEEP Cleaning process we will move from top to bottom, room to room.

CUAY Essentials:

The following are some of the basics needed in setting the stage for CUAYing. Be sure to link us at CUAY.org or on social media @cuaylife so we can share any new natural and eco-safe products to add to your cleaning closet. For now, we will stick to the old faithfuls.

- Bleach
- Pine Sol
- Broom and Dustpan on each floor or side of home if possible
- Paper Towels
- Vinegar (natural antimicrobial) great for glass and mirrors

- Bowl or bucket for soap water and mopping
- Mop
- Cloths and sponges for scrubbing

Please note that inhaling harsh chemicals for long periods can be toxic. Be sure to deep clean in a well-ventilated area (open your windows) or use face coverings and take breaks while deep cleaning. PS. Never mix any chemicals while cleaning! It is toxic and harmful to inhale.

Let's dive into the DEEP Cleaning.

Kitchen:

Sink Science

Before you start CUAYing in the kitchen, you have to run some dishwater. Hopefully, there aren't any dishes in the sink, to begin with. Either way, you need to sanitize your kitchen sink. Spray it down with an antibacterial spray and make sure your sink is washed, scrubbed down, and rinsed out well. Then start running your warm soapy water. My mother always kept a small glass at the back of her sink with bleach in it, which would save time for sanitizing the kitchen throughout the day. Always run your dishwater as hot as you can stand it and add your favorite dishwashing liquid and a dash of liquid bleach. This will be your base for deep cleaning the kitchen. If the water gets cold or dirty over time just drain it, clean the sink again from leftover debris, and run a fresh batch of dishwater to continue your kitchen cleaning. At the end of each day, the sink should be cleaned out and any old food in the drain disposed of.

Refrigerator

The refrigerator is the heart of the kitchen and should remain organized and clean. This means you have to be mindful to sanitize your refrigerator shelves often, at least weekly. If your family does leftovers, then you should invest in airtight-stackable storage containers. I prefer to use compartmental storage containers so that we can have full meals ready to be warmed quickly.

Now that you already have your soapy dishwater ready to use. Start by removing all items from the refrigerator or take it shelf by shelf. Soap up a cloth and wipe down all shelves and surfaces in the refrigerator. Remember to clean out the door and wipe all condiments containers down as well. And don't forget to check those ingredients too, collect all items with artificial flavors, colors, sweeteners, and weird preservatives that you can't spell and drop them into the trashcan on your way to the sink. You may have to go back to the sink for another dip if your cloth gets soiled or dry while cleaning but it's all good, that's what progress looks like. Make note of all the items that you CUAYed away and find healthy replacements at your local health food store.

Stove

Gas or electric, keeping your stove and oven clean adds to the overall cleanliness of your kitchen. An unclean stove is a sign of a nasty kitchen, so before you start prepping a meal or snack for your family be sure to clean the stove. When you're finished, no sign of yesterday's meals should linger. That goes for the top of the stove as well as inside the oven. If you spill something in the oven while baking, stop and wipe it up immediately. Hot messes are best cleaned up before they cool off. That works in the kitchen and in life, might I add.

If you have anything that you leave on the stove like a water kettle or utensil holder, be sure you clean those items thoroughly as well.

Cabinets

First and foremost, always make sure your cabinets and hardware are sturdy and secure. If they aren't, find a way to stabilize them. Call your local handyman or handywoman to help you out or research a Do-It-Yourself remedy for loose kitchen cabinets. Having stable cabinets is important aesthetically because you will appreciate your kitchen more if you like how it looks. No matter what size your kitchen is, you will have to divide up cabinet space to organize what you have. The basic sections may include cookware, plates

and bowls, cups and glasses, dry foods, and my favorite...
the spice cabinet. Wipe down you cabinets often as they tend
to get sticky.

Spice Cabinet or Seasoning

This is one of my favorite places in the kitchen because what
you find here will really tell you a lot about the family. Sea
salt versus iodized salt, black versus cracked pepper. Do
your spices contain MSG? Or any of its other names? You
might have to do a little research. Do you have additives in
your spices that add flavor using chemicals? CUAY them to
the trash. Your spices should be just that, SPICES. No added
junk to build up in your system and cause disease. One day
we won't have to read ingredients so closely to make sure
we aren't killing ourselves softly with non-foods that are
added to our food supply. But for now, they are still FDA
approved and on our grocery aisles. So, we have to be extra
cautious. #ReadtheLabels

Dry Foods/Pantry

As with the spice cabinet, the secret to CUAY your dry food
cabinet is to discard any unnatural ingredients. Anything
with high fructose corn syrup*, dyes, monosodium
glutamate (MSG*), excessive artificial flavors, or hard to
read preservatives should be limited and ultimately

eliminated* from your kitchen. Categorize items and similarly sized boxes so it is easier for you to find things.

Canned foods should also be limited and avoided when possible. Vegetables especially are generally high in sodium from the can and sitting in water for extended periods, sometimes years reduces the amount of actual nutrients for your consumption. Buy fresh or frozen vegetables instead if you can't keep up with using fresh produce. Don't forget to wipe down all shelves from dust and food particles to reduce the risk of attracting pests.

Freezer

Speaking of storing frozen food - how's your refrigerator freezer looking? When's the last time you gave it a deep clean? The freezer in most homes gets neglected when it comes to kitchen clean-up so don't feel bad if your answers to the above questions are "I don't know" or "never."

Begin deep cleaning your freezer by throwing away everything you can't immediately identify. All those freezer bags with items you can't recall, just let it go! In your freshly organized kitchen, all bagged freezer items will be labeled with contents and the storage date.

When it comes to freezer times, I like to follow the "Liquid Gold" rule. What's Liquid Gold? Well, it's a nutrient-based primary food with natural antioxidants* and antibiotics initially produced by women for the consumption of their newborn babies. Yes, breast milk! As a mother of two with over 2 years of nursing under my belt, successfully freezing your supply is crucial. My midwife's rule of grace for breast milk is four hours on the counter, four days in the refrigerator, and four months in the freezer. Of-course each food item could differ a bit however in general, after about four (but no more than six months) of storing anything in the freezer, if you haven't rotated it out by now, circulate it on to the trash. Seriously.

After that, go ahead and organize whatever is left in the freezer. Meats should be stored together as well as vegetables, fruits, and any other category of food. While organizing, take the hot soapy cloth from your already prepped sink, and sanitize all surfaces in the freezer. The cloth must be hot to avoid it sticking.

Microwave

If you're going to use it, at least keep it clean, and be sure to use a microwave splatter guard for each use to reduce the need to clean it so frequently. You will still need to keep the base crumb and grime free and throw the splatter guard in the dishwasher biweekly or so depending on use. Use your sanitized dishwater to clean all surfaces in the microwave. Consider carefully removing the glass tray in order to soak it in the sink for deep cleaning. Rinse, Dry, and replace it in the microwave.

The outside of the microwave also deserves some attention. The buttons and handle need to be wiped daily to maintain kitchen cleanliness.

The microwave works by heating up the water molecules inside the food. If you pay attention to cooked food before and after being microwaved, you may notice microwave heat is different and research shows that it's not the best form of heat to depend on. We are here to talk about cleaning but when possible, avoid or limit microwaving food. Even if we wanted to stay completely away from exposure to it, we would have a hard time. Most restaurant kitchens use it to some degree. And then there's your neighbor.

Silverware and Dishware

If you don't have a full set of silverware, fret not. Keep them clean and at least sorted so that they are easily identified. That is the main goal. Some kitchens have tons of silverware that have accumulated over the years. This leads to junky silverware drawers and makes it difficult to find specific items like the wine opener or your favorite cereal spoon. Just because you had it forever doesn't mean you need to keep it forever. Seriously, who needs 10 spatulas or 25 spoons? A chef maybe, but I'm sure they even have their favorite few. So, minimize your cooking utensils too, so you always know where to find what you're looking for.

Dishes

For active families, having breakable dishware can be hazardous or at least costly to constantly replace. Luckily there are plastic, BPA-free, dishwasher friendly dishes that can be used instead. Having fancy china is nice for special occasions but not as common for most families nowadays, so use what fits your family.

The question is, when is the special occasion? Did you have a special occasion this year? What about last year, did you pull the good dishes out then? Well, you know where I'm headed with this... you got it: Let it go! Sell them, share them, use them for anger management in the backyard, gather the mess and move on. If you haven't used them much, the likelihood that your family china will be used or even coveted in future generations is even slimmer.

To my coffee lovers and tea-aholics, I know you love a new mug. But how many mugs do you really need? Regift a few or donate the old ones to maximize your cabinet space for other items. Some of us have dishware that hasn't seen dishwater in years, just sitting on cabinet shelves looking pretty but never in use. Let's move past the need to hoard and choose the organization instead.

Pots and Pans

Repeat after me: Stainless steel or NO DEAL. Please be mindful of what you are cooking in. Properly maintained cast iron, glass, and stoneware cooking pots are great also. But none of that faux stainless or any other black-coated pots or pans.

If your kitchen is stocked with anything other than the above mentioned, do your family a favor and put them into the trash pile. The health risks on our body and brain are just not worth it. Traditionalists would agree that everything new isn't good for you. When our family first moved to a new state, we had to find cookware locally, and luckily, we found affordable stainless-steel pots right at the thrift store. So, give that a try.

Now that you have your lovely stainless-steel pots and pans, make sure you store them neatly in your cabinet. Start with the largest size and stack them on top of each other with the lids accessible inside or to the side. Same for all bowls and bakeware. The goal is to open your storage cabinet and have a home for all supplies, not a mountain of who-knows-what under your sink. After pots and pans are cleaned and ready to be stored their appropriate location will be waiting for them.

Trashcan

No matter if you have the no-touch trash can or the traditional step pedal one, ever so often it will need a deep cleaning. This means it needs to be sanitized inside and out. Most trash cans have sludge at the bottom that has either seeped through the bag overtime or missed the bag altogether and has been sitting there waiting for a deep clean ever since.

You should be a professional at running water for sanitizing by now. Hot soapy water with bleach **or** Pine-Sol will due. Taking the can outside to be cleaned might work best or you could use a bowl to transfer water into the can. Letting it set for a while typically helps to loosen any hardened grime from the bottom, but it may still need to be scrubbed. You can use a long mop or broom handle with a cloth or thick paper towel attached to scrub the bottom of the can.

The lid of the can needs care too. You may notice food debris under the lid so clean and scrub that as well along with the outside of the trashcan. This is a deep cleaning and daily CUAY task as the top of the trashcan gets dirty throughout the week. Or you may be like my mother, who doesn't like keeping a kitchen trash can and just reuses grocery bags and throws trash out as needed. No overnight trash lingering in her kitchen. Again, it is up to you how often to deep clean certain parts of your home. You can choose a part of your home each weekend or do it all every weekend. But DEEP cleaning is a must at the start and during your CUAYing journey.

Kitchen Cracks

All those places where food may fall and be forgotten. You know how you drop it and say, "I'll get that later." Well, it's later and the deep cleaning step is the perfect time to get to it. Between countertops and appliances is the area that bothers me the most. Now is the time to move those appliances out and sweep and/or mop there efficiently.

Bathrooms:

Toilets

Toilets have lots of crevices and I recommend that you deep clean the bathroom first and often. Around the base, behind, under the seat, and at the hinge where the lid opens,and shuts should all be thoroughly sanitized. Not to mention the toilet seat handle that carries the most germs. Another commonly missed area is the front base where dribbles dry into long stains. Also, spray down and sanitize where the bolts of the toilet are, and crud builds quickly.

Honestly, every time someone uses the bathroom, they should be wiping the seat off after themselves. Ladies that means you too. Shhh. We don't like to admit it, but we dribble sometimes on the seat as well. Especially under the seat. It only takes a few extra squares of toilet paper to clean the toilet after you're done.

Ultimately everyone is responsible for cleaning the bathroom daily. Each week there should be a "toilet deep cleaning" on someone's radar, to be sure all the crevices are clear from weekly nastiness.

The toilet really is a throne. Without it, we would be using the bathroom outside but most of us can't recall those days other than in books or movies. We have to keep in mind that each human should be eliminating their bowels at least once a day. Twice is even better. So, with that much waste circulating through your bathroom, you should be sanitizing it daily to make sure no yuckiness is transmitted outside of the bathroom or between family members. Germs can easily be tracked into your living room or kitchen area if everyone isn't mindful about cleaning up after each visit.

The master bathroom is off-limits to children in our home. Being responsible for the mess in their own bathroom helps them to notice how the master bathroom stays cleaner.

Sinks

Keeping your sinks clean is imperative to keeping a clean home altogether. From the bathroom to the kitchen sink, we should be looking for clean and dry surfaces. We talked about sanitizing the kitchen sink before tidying the kitchen.

The same goes for the bathroom sinks. That gunk that builds up behind the bathroom facet is soap scum and dirt. It happens so fast but just think of the scum you cannot see with your eyes. No need to be a germaphobe, because all bacteria aren't bad and no, we're not here to live in a completely sterile environment or live in a bubble. But who wants the same hands that just flushed the toilet to be picking through the refrigerator for a snack?

If our sinks and faucets are not deep cleaned and kept that way, then there is no telling what we take from our sinks to our mouths or out into the rest of the world. Practice wiping around your sink after each use. This means drying off the area and making sure no liquid soap dribbles are around the sink or left inside. We'll get into CUAYing in public bathrooms later...

Bathtubs/Showers

Baths are healing. The skin is the largest organ of the body. It absorbs and emits secretions via sweat. It is porous and lively. In a bath the pores open and we can use that vulnerable state to absorb nutrient-rich* herbs or vitamins directly into our system and nourish and cleanse ourselves during bath time.

Whether you are taking a soaking bath or a steamy shower, after all that lovely bathing there's a memory left behind. It's called scum. My son loves baths. He'll soak for an hour, but when it's time to come out he often has to be reminded that he shouldn't leave his dirt behind. All the dirt that was released from the skin can be found hovering around the rim of the tub or the sides and bottom of your shower. When the water is turned off or drained the dirt sticks to the sides and for baths, it creates a nice ring around the tub at the exact water level of the bath.

It's usually oily and has to be cleaned immediately or it makes the cleaning way harder to handle in the future. Hopefully, your tub doesn't hold memories of passed baths left behind. But if it does today is the day to knock that out and set new expectations for your family moving forward. No rings left behind is the goal.

Besides rings, the rim of the bathtub can also get nasty with old soap stains, conditioner bottle rings, etc. I've even seen some homes that have washcloths laid along the edge to dry out for the next use. No thanks. If you don't have a towel rack in your bathroom or in the bathtub area to hold all the washcloths for your family, find another solution. Towel racks are an inexpensive tool and there are adhesive hooks to stick to the shower or be drilled into the bathroom wall. If that is outside of your budget use a few medium-sized nails hammered into the wall, one for each family member. Those nail holes will need to be filled if you want to upgrade the bathroom with a towel rack at some point, but it's better than having your damp towels on the floor or random places around the house.

To deep clean your shower/bathtub, start by spraying down the dirty areas, then run some soapy water in the tub, add bleach or cleaner of choice and get your scrub on. Remember to clean showerheads and any shower racks when you're deep cleaning also. They hardly get cleaning attention otherwise.

"SAVE OUR SHOWER" (SOS)

I rented a home with a beautiful garden tub and a separate shower. The homeowners that we rented from must have never cleaned the shower. It was a beautiful home, and we were grateful to live there, the shower was just a major eyesore. It was caked with what seemed to be years of dirt build-up ingrained in the base of the shower.

My mother came to visit after my son was born and when she saw my shower, she looked at me sideways as if to say, "I know I raised you better than that."

I had to quickly explain that it was hand-me-down dirt from before I moved in. We'd been there for a few months and I was too big and pregnant to get down on my knees to scrub while I inhaled strong chemicals, so I sprayed and used a long brush. It still wouldn't wash clean.

My mother wouldn't take my, "nothing works" reason for a final answer and she said, "Let me see."

She used cleaning powder, soap, and bleach to create a paste in the bottom. She let it sit for a while, then scrubbed it vigorously. The buildup washed away like it was never there. I was amazed and felt so much more comfortable showering without someone else's old dirt under my feet.

If you have a will to get something clean, odds are there is a way. If it can't be scrubbed clean the tub may need to be resurfaced, especially in older homes. But there is a way. And bathing in someone else's fossilized dirt, or even your own, can't be the only way. Go take a look. Does your shower need saving too? Deep clean it and then give the family a tour of the upgraded expectations. CUAY all day.

Mirrors

With a culture of selfies plaguing the planet, we get to see loads of bathroom mirrors. Why are they often so dirty? Looking at yourself through clouded mirrors must be symbolic of how you view yourself.

Vinegar is actually the best mirror cleaner. There are cleaners infused* with vinegar now, but you can also mix your own and cut it with water. Vinegar is good because it sanitizes and usually doesn't leave streaks as water alone would. So, before you catch the right light and angle for your next mirror pic, clean that mirror from that toothpaste splatter from this morning and that oil sheen spritz from last week. We want to see you better.

Corners:

Start by using a broom to clean those ceiling corners that are most often missed. You may need to wear a pair of shades or eyewear to protect yourself from the falling dust. Clean all ceiling corners first around the house or in each room as you go. Some people like to clean the whole house at the same time. I'm one of those people. It looks like a tornado until you are nearing the end of deep cleaning when it all starts to come together.

Make sure to clean the corners of the floor as well. You will likely have to move furniture and get behind large pieces. DO IT. If you need help, stop and find the best way to move things without hurting yourself. Get a neighbor, call someone to assist, or plan ahead for extra help. Two is better than one. There are even sliders you can purchase that go under the corners of large pieces of furniture that you can use to move them more easily. The key is to plan it out.

Culturally, corners are always seen as the first step in cleaning your home. Grandma and them used to say, "keep them corners clear because negative energy can build up and live there." After becoming a homeowner, myself, I always noticed how spiders can creep into your corners and build a dwelling of their own if you aren't mindful to keep the dust and debris down.

Carpeted areas sometimes need the corners swept if your vacuum can't reach them. Keep that in mind and swipe the corners before you get started.

Remember when checking corners off your deep cleaning list, you should be checking corners outside around your home too. You can sweep them down or have your home pressure washed periodically to make sure even your outside corners are clean and clear.

Walls:

Walls get overlooked a lot. However, they can be most unsightly when they are dirty and have grim and dust on them. Do yourself a favor. If walls are too dirty, hit the reset button and just paint them. That would be another DIY for recommendations. But to clean walls make sure you have paint that isn't damaged when wiped down. Try a sample area to test.

Be sure you are not using any bleach that could change the color of your current paint. I recommend using the "Magic Erase" from Mr. Clean. It works pretty well. Otherwise, some good old soap and water will do the trick.

Areas of the wall around light switches and outlets get dirty too. As well as walls down the steps or any other active area of the home. Once you prepare yourself with supplies and take a deep look at your walls, I'm sure you will see spots that you may have never thought would get so dirty. Look and you will find. This is a good task for children. It helps them to build a mindset to watch where their hands go when they get up from the table or walk around the house. If they know it'll be their chore later, they are more inclined to pay attention to it. They may even start regulating others for putting their hands on the walls as well. Let's just call it, social accountability.

Crevices:

Cleaning crevices* earns you deep cleaning bonus points. Decide on a time frame for each area to be tended to directly and frequently. For your home, this could mean weekly, bi-monthly, or even daily depending on the usage.

Window Seals

Even if you don't open your windows often, but especially if you do, you need to clean out the window seals and clear out bugs or possible moisture building up there. Also, if you have a habit of storing things in your window seals consider finding another home for those items or minimize what is left there.

Door Frames

We just open it and close it, but how often do we clean around our door or wipe the knobs off? Take the time to do it now! Lubricate your door hinges if needed and be sure there and doors leading to the outside have a good seal and no air is coming in or going out. This keeps your electric bill down and your home temperature regulated. Do the same for window seals.

Laundry Room Lint Traps

Clearing out lint traps in your dryer is good for fire safety purposes. If you're a grill master or firepit connoisseur, you already know that lint from your dryer can kindle a flame nicely. Of course, we are not interested in kindling that in our laundry rooms.

Be mindful to empty your lint trap out after every load to avoid build-up. Have a professional deep clean the dryer air vent annually to avoid possible fire dangers. Locate a local professional to help you deep clean your laundry room vents and set a reminder on your devices to have them back out next year. Meanwhile, get your household into the habit of removing lint after each use. #FireFightersDaughter

For Kitchen Crevices

See Kitchen Section.

Floors:

My oh my. Floors might be the hardest part of CUAYing. It is literally a never-ending job. But deep cleaning them isn't so bad, only because it doesn't have to be done every day. Depending on your floor type and square footage, you can usually get it done within an hour or so. Start off by clearing the floor from any moveable items that could prevent you from cleaning the floor underneath. Or at least minimize anything in the way of the floor, (dining chairs, throw rugs, trash cans, shoes, etc.)

Floors will be done last when cleaning because this is where all the dust and trash will settle after you deep clean. When the time comes go from corner to corner and sweep up trash when cleaning tile, wood, or any non-carpet floor. You'll have to sweep it more than once to really get the dirt and dust up. If you are vacuuming remember that most vacuums do not get all the way to the edge of the carpet. In this case, you will have to sweep out the corners and sides of the walls before you vacuum.

Sweeping

Don't bother sweeping it all in a big pile. You could make several piles, or you may need to carry the dustpan around with you. I like to call it the "L sweep" because you literally sweep around the room in an "L" shape. This means you sweep from in front of you into the dustpan and then to the right/or left of you into the dustpan. Then you move to another place and repeat until you have covered the entire floor surface. I know you may want to use a vacuum to do this part. But I have found in my cleaning experience that using a vacuum on hard surfaces often just blow dust around. So, unless you have a High-tech vacuum that can efficiently sweep hard floors, it is best to just stick to the faithful broom and dustpan.

Tile

For tile floors, you will have to sweep times two. Yeah, times two. The first sweep is for dirt and the second one is for whatever you missed the first time. If you have a robot sweeper that'll work too.

Then comes the mopping. Pine-Sol is my favorite mop bucket ingredient because of its fresh scent and cleansing power. In most cases, it won't harm the finishing on your floors, but be sure to test it out on a small area before you go all in. Deep cleaning will not eliminate all of your tile issues in that it may not clean grout. There are specific solutions if that is one of your concerns.

Wood

Red oak, hickory, maple, or cherry. Wood floors add a warm feeling to your home or space. But they need a little extra love to stay warm and cozy instead of dust piled splinter givers. Your double sweep is a part of your daily CUAYing and starts off your deep cleaning. There are various cleaners that can be used, but I have found that Pine-Sol is an affordable and effective way to clean and mop wood floors.

Be sure not to drown your wood with water or cleaner. It will damage them. But you can still mop by using a damp map and cleaner to get the job done. On occasion, your wood floors will also need good waxing to keep up the shine and grain consistency. Your flooring can look great and last for a very long time if you keep up with the maintenance. The wax will help to keep them sealed from water damage and shined nicely from the scuffs of the days in-between.

Carpet

My main complaint about carpet is that it traps dust and dirt so deep that it eventually needs to be shampooed out. You can vacuum or sweep up surface debris but the dirt that seeps into the carpet will not come out all the way. Carpet holds dust, dirt, and dead skin and has been known to cause allergies if not well maintained.

If you're wondering why you, a guest or a loved one experiences sinus issues in your house, it could be due to your cleanliness, especially if you have carpet. It needs to be shampooed to be fully deep cleaned and unfortunately, there's really no way around it. You can spot clean high traffic areas when you CUAY, but you will still need to either rent or buy a shampooer or hire someone to shampoo and deep clean your carpet a couple of times a year to keep them refreshed. It's the price you pay for having plushness under your feet.

Again, floors will need ongoing cleaning throughout the week. So, make it a habit to sweep around the edges of your carpeted rooms before you vacuum. You will need to vacuum often to minimize the dust and dirt buildup in your home. Check out that filter and vacuum bag to see all the history you captured in the form of dust. Amazing right.

PETS:

Owning a pet is extremely rewarding. They love you even if you smell bad or have a bad attitude. But maintaining a living space with a pet is also a huge responsibility. It's hard to understand why people call themselves pet parents until you have one. From feeding, shedding to scooping their waste pet owners have to keep an eye out for cleaning or your home can quickly turn into a barnyard.

Cleaning up after your pet is much like cleaning up after yourself. You have to monitor where your pet goes and what they do so you are able to clean up after them quickly. Even a drinking bowl for little puppies can turn into a mess.

A few splashes from the bowl turn into dirty paw prints all over the floors. It happens so fast. Even if you mopped and cuayed your home this morning, it can be frustrating to see how easy it is ruined in the afternoon when pets are involved.

The best way to cuay for a pet is to think ahead. Instead of leaving that bowl on the floor where you know splashes will cause a problem, place the bowl on an absorbent surface so the splashes don't make it to the floor at all, like a towel or mat. My most valuable tip for pet owners is to plan ahead. Once you know the pattern of your pet, you'll develop solutions to keep their path as clean as possible.

Pet hair though, is a different story. It's an ongoing battle to keep shedding pet hair and dander to a minimum when you have a furry family member. Reduce shedding by using a grooming* tool a few times a week to get off excess hair. Grooming tools are great because they gently eject loose hair so you can comb it off into a pile. However, you'll still need to sweep frequently and vacuum furniture where they leave lingering hair behind. It's a service of love. Care for your pet with a smile, understanding that it's in exchange for the authentic love they give in return.

Puppy Parents

Please CUAY after your dogs and scoop their poop. Understandably, it is not the most exciting part of puppy ownership, but it is necessary. When you scoop for your dog you help cut down on the transmission of disease and you save others from stepping in it, inhaling it, or struggling with their dog to stop sniffing your dog's leftover poop. Beware of the dog whistleblowers. Those neighbors that watch to see if you are going to scoop after your pet. You should be able to hold yourself accountable for taking care of your responsibility as a pet owner.

Also, if you are conscious of the environment, it is best to use a biodegradable bag. And if you're not a fan of feeling the warmth through the bag or believe that bacteria can seep through the bag and contaminate your hands, try investing in a bagged scooper for a no-touch scooping experience.

Counter/Tabletops:

For most families, more surface space just means more clutter. It is imperative to make sure that all table tops only have on them what belongs. I am so guilty of this one. I pile things on counters and forget to CUAY all the time. Before I close the downstairs and head up nowadays, I have to circle back to all the counters and tables to gather everything I left behind. You will notice misplaced items immediately when you do a walkthrough. Find a real home for belongings that are usually left on tabletops and leave only what you want to look at when you scan the scene.

Bedrooms:

Closets

Every week on laundry day, we should train ourselves to let go of clothes we no longer need. If it doesn't look right, fit your body or style anymore: let it go. This way faded and overused pieces can be discarded before they even reach the closet. BUT, once it's in the closet, oftentimes things not worn are buried and hidden.

Find a useful way to organize your closet so that you can find pieces without creating daily stress for yourself. My sister taught me to separate work clothes from personal clothes, but I like to take it a step further and organize by color. I always start with blacks at the beginning and then flow through the color cycle from red to violet with whites at the end.

Organizing shoes could be a book of its own. I'll just sum it up here with one valuable tip: buy what you can store. If you don't have room to store another pair of shoes sufficiently in your closet, give some away before you go shopping. Notify your "pass-it-on crew" to come to get a bag or donate them.

There are many different shoe storage options from storage bins to shoe mounts. Find your style and set up your closet the right way. Remember, every pair of shoes must have a home. Boots together, sneakers together, sandals together, heels together, and so on. The organization style is endless. It's your preference, sort by color, style ,or season, just do what works for you.

If you live in a climate with multiple seasons you should be packing and storing one season's clothes and preparing your closet for the upcoming season. Stick to annual occasions to help keep your family on schedule. The seasons change most around two main times of the year: The Spring Equinox* and Fall Equinox* (March 22nd and September 22nd respectively). These are the days of the year that are equal in day and night. After March 22nd the days lengthen until we reach peak daylight hours on June 22nd during the Summer Solstice and Summer officially begins. The days begin to shorten after the Fall Equinox on September 22nd until winter officially begins on December 22nd. If you are not familiar with these times of the year. I highly recommend continuing your research for full clarity. These are nature's time clocks and great times to DEEP CLEAN your home and turn over your closet and seasonal decor.

Dresser Drawers

My mother couldn't stand messy dressers on top, but especially inside the dresser drawers. Dare I ask her where a piece of my clothing was and she came in my room to see all my drawers stuffed with jumbled-up, wrinkled clothes. She would get so fed up that she would empty out everything from my drawers onto the middle of the floor and make me refold and organize everything again. I guess I wasn't a natural CUAYer as a teenager.

Although her method seemed extreme at the time, she programmed in me a need to have tidy dresser drawers. I later realized it actually makes getting dressed easier because things are easier to find and don't need to be ironed.

If we could hang up everything, folding clothes would be irrelevant. But then again, we'd have to have extra-large closets built in every home. We're not quite there yet around the globe. Some people don't even have drawers, so forget a closet to maintain. Let that marinate for a minute.

At least find a way to fold and/or roll the items in your drawers to save you from stressful mornings, wrinkled clothes, or worse, the *"Mommy Hurricane"*. That's what it looked like after my mom would come through to "help" me organize my dresser drawers. Next time you open your dresser drawers and see things in disarray, imagine the breeze speeding up in your room because the *"Mommy Hurricane"* is on its way straight to you.

Beds

Did you make your bed this morning? Well, if you didn't, you're among the majority. Studies found that only 37% of American adults make their beds in the morning. Meaning that the majority of adults leave their covers in shambles. What do you think that percentage is for children? Why has this turned into a norm in our society? I am a habitual bed maker. It's the first thing I do after using the bathroom. But for some people, it is not even a thought. Many think, "What's the point? I'm going to get back in it later today." However, when it comes to cleaning up after yourself, fixing your bed is one of the first tasks of your day. If this book does nothing else, I hope it gets families to respect their sleep space more and at least start making their beds in the mornings.

Mattresses

To deep clean your bed, you need to have a weekly schedule of changing your bedsheets. After a week of sleeping, sweating and whatever else, you need to take time to hit the reset button for dreamworld. I always recommend families using a mattress pad to cover the actual mattress when possible. This will help preserve the longevity* of your mattress and prevent stains and the mattress pad can easily be removed and washed as needed.

Prop your mattress on its side and give it a good beating after you remove the sheets to remove the dirt and dust left behind. Note: Always take a moment to check the creases of your mattress. Surely you know, bugs are creepers. Make sure there are no bug stains or bug activity on your mattress and sheets on linen wash day.

Mattresses are much heavier than they used to be. So, moving it to beat the dust out may be cumbersome. If your vacuum has a hose, try vacuuming your bed periodically instead. You can also spray your mattress with a disinfecting spray between washes to freshen it up. And of course, when you rise in the morning say a new daily prayer while you make your bed.

There are many ways to spruce up a bed. The most common way is to lay all the layers flat with the fitted sheet tucked and top sheet laid flat, spread your comforter or blanket on top of your bed end to end. Fluff your pillows and cover them with the comforter or lean them against the headboard. You can be as precise as you would like with your turndown style. As long as you make it appear neat and inviting. Someone special lays their head there at night. Treat that space accordingly, it's sacred.

Pillow talk

What about your pillows? Do you wash them? How often do you replace them? Be sure to add pillows to the list of items to spray down with disinfectant spray during your weekly sheet transitions. You can beat them to fluff and if your pillows look extra soiled, try washing them when possible. If they are not refreshed after a wash, toss and replace them instead. Some pillows may not be washable, so check the care instructions and proceed with caution. Make sure your pillows pass the smell test before you lay your head down. If they fail, you have a bed to make.

Around the House:

Artwork

If your walls are bare and you don't have any artwork up, here's a friendly reminder to support an artist and bless your walls with something beautiful, unique, and creative. If you already have artwork up on your walls, ask yourself how often you clean them. You don't need to use any chemicals; a weekly dusting will suffice. But don't just let your artwork sit there month after month without attention. #ArtFan

Here are a few suggestions of artists to support if you're interested

@Nathanjalanitaylor   **@justincopeland_art**

@DSDpainting   **@rfordtheartist**

@PiecesofCeeKay

Electronics

It doesn't matter if your television is mounted or on a stand. The real question is, when's the last time you dusted it or cleaned the screen? Many of us have grown accustomed to watching our shows through all the smudged fingerprints.

Whether you are using isopropyl alcohol, white vinegar, and water, glass cleaner, or plain water, make sure you are using a soft cloth and slight pressure to gently clean your devices. Remember not to spray the electronics directly. Spray the cloth and use that to clean appropriately.

The same goes for any other devices around the house: laptops, iPads, tablets, speaker systems, and gaming units. They all need to be cleaned periodically. Dust is very harmful to electronics over time, so keeping them clean and dust-free will actually add to their longevity.

Cell phones

You may be thinking, "How can I CUAY my cell phone?" Well, there are actually multiple ways to clean your smart device. The first being physical cleaning. Using an approved sanitizing liquid, remove the case, and use a clean cloth or paper towel to wipe your naked phone. It doesn't get a daily cleaning like you hopefully do so all the germs that it has encountered have had time to accumulate. All the germs from that trip to the bathroom, those selfies in the mall, that stranger you let take a picture of you on date night are still present. Of course, you'll want to disinfect all your cases along with the device as well. Be sure to perform this disinfection somewhere safe, where a fall won't cause you to have a cracked screen or damaged device. NEVER spray the device directly. Spray a cloth and wipe it down thoroughly. Depending on your cell phone usage you should make cleaning a habit every few days or at least weekly.

Storage Spaces

Garages, storage rooms, attics, and even the infamous junk drawer in your kitchen can be eyesores in a well-kept home. For many families, their entire home is 95% organized and then there's the storage space at 0%. So where do you start? How can you get a hold of your storage space to begin the process? You simply work the CUAY program. Follow the same steps that you used to get the rest of your home in order.

The biggest hurdle will be letting go of what you don't really need from your storage space, then finding adequate storage for what's left. Whether you use bins, shelves, itemized grouping, or whatever you prefer, making it a functional space with room to grow is the goal. But remember that everything must be DEEP cleaned. Yes, even your jam-packed storage space needs to be cleaned out and organized. If you can't see what's going on in there and you never use the space, then just pay someone to come trash or donate it all and save yourself the hassle of sorting and sharing. Purge* the space out and start over.

Lighting

Ceiling fans, lampshades, LEDs, fluorescent, neon, regardless of what you have in your home, the fixtures and supporting materials need to be deep cleaned on the regular. Of course, this is electricity so we don't want to use water, but dusting is a must.

Often when you remove the bowls around standard lights you will find dead bugs and dust. This will worsen over time so handle it now and keep it up. Lighting is the centerpiece of your home; they bring light into our world so we should clean them properly. Let's not take our lighting for granted by allowing the dust to collect.

Living Room

I can still remember as a little girl spending the night on someone's couch and not being able to sleep because the couch smelled like ass! No other way to put it. It was super funky, and I always thought to myself, "When I get a house, my couch will not be stinky. I'll be sure of it." But other than actively making sure my children don't pass gas while sitting on the couch and that no one sits there without clothes on, the only way to be sure I don't turn into the dreaded "stinky couch house" is to clean it often.

Everything in my house gets the sniff test. Especially my couch. To keep furniture and other furniture clean I always start with limiting access to food there. Meaning no eating on the couch for starters aside from the occasional popcorn for movie night. Otherwise, it's a hard "no" to having food on the couch. Somehow, crumbs, dust, and debris still find their way into the crevices and I have to figure out a way to clean it depending on the couch style. Luckily, our current couch has recliners and all the mess that typically would gather under the cushions now just falls to the floor so we can conveniently see when it's gross and dusty when we recline.

If your couch is more stationary, you will have to lift the cushions and sweep underneath instead. If your cushions aren't moveable, another option is to get the vacuum hose down in the crevices. I like listening intentionally to hear the sound of the vacuum sucking up debris and doing its job. It sounds so rewarding. Like it's a fight and I'm saying, "I gotcha dirt!"

Externally, a light wipe with water and Pine-Sol mixture does the trick topically to refresh the surfaces of most furniture. Again, test it on small areas before you use it. The cloth should be damp, not drenched – you don't need to soak the furniture.

Base your living room furniture cleaning on the texture of the couch and deep clean everything specifically to suit those needs.

Bookshelves

Hopefully, you still have some paper books in your home. Especially if you have children in the house. Digital books are a great way to carry your bookshelf around with you. But ultimately, the joy of flipping through the pages and smelling the scent of print is priceless. Being able to highlight the pages, underline the text and write notes in the margins. Ahhh, the beauty of a good ol' book.

Though I'm a hardcopy book lover, I'll be sure to make this one available for my digital book lovers as well. But if that device crashes or the internet is down, make sure you have a copy of <u>CUAY</u> on your bookshelf as well. You never know when you might need a hands-on reminder.

No matter how many books you have on your shelf, be sure to give them regular attention. Dust them off and place them back in their home on the shelf when not in use, and absolutely do not leave any pages folded after reading. #LibraryTreatment #HomeLibrary

Desk

Working from home is more popular these days and it helps to have a separate space for work-related items apart from typical home life. But CUAYing for your office desk is the same whether it is a home office or corporate office.

Start by sorting the items on your desk. You likely won't have things to share from your office, so prioritizing will be the goal instead. Organize the piles on your desk and make a to-do list based on a need's assessment or any approaching deadlines. There are numerous apps available on your computer or smart device so find the one that works best for you to help organize your list and support you with reminders and motivation until you reach completion.

Keep your desk free from dust, food trash, and other clutter. Leave a note behind for yourself when you shut down your office space after a day's work. Maybe a note of encouragement. Maybe a note of accountability or just a note of first things to focus on when you get back to your space. When you come in for your next work session read the note and dispose of it or add it to your to-do list. The goal is not to have a desk full of notes without clear direction.

Dusting

Dust is the devil. Not really, it's just one of those things you are going to have to face at some point. Depending on the surfaces in your home you will need various dusting methods. Wood, vinyl, books, chairs, lampshades, and so many other types. Find the right product to clean with or create your own to help cut down on the dust, especially if you have people visiting or in the home with allergies. Keeping the dust down can help keep them from getting sinus infections or having sneezing spells or itchy eyes.

Growing up my mother would have us dust and deep clean every Saturday morning. Before we could watch cartoons or even eat our morning cereal, we'd have to dust the infamous wall unit. You know that home furniture from the '80s where all the collectibles lived. Thankfully, those aren't as popular and modern homes have minimal surface area and trinkets. But those pesky TV stands, bookshelves, lighting fixtures will still need weekly dusting.

While you're at it: When's the last time you changed the air filter in your home? Enhance your air quality by changing the filter according to your system's recommendations. The dust that builds up and traps old air in our homes can get pretty nasty when left unchecked. Basically, until we live in naturally ventilated homes like *Earthship Biotecture*, we'll have to abide by the air filter rules and keep dusting as a primary task in our deep cleaning rotation.

Purifying your Air

We've covered the entire house, top to bottom but we missed something in between. How do you clean your air? Airing your home out is one of the oldest cleaning tips I witnessed growing up. The open windows will improve your home's air quality by removing stuffy, stale air and circulating fresh air. Opening your windows and doors to allow air to flow freely will help everyone breathe easier. Be mindful of pollen during certain times of the year, but even your allergy-prone family members will benefit from the breeze.

Traditional Options for Purifying the Air
-White Sage* for burning
-Incense Frankincense, Yang Ylang, Nag Champa, Pacchiol.

These are some of the traditional fragrances that typically leave a soft and intentional scent behind instead of a burned wood smell like some cheaper off-brand incense. If you smell burned wood, go ahead and make a mental note of the brand and CUAY it to the trash. The above-mentioned scents are more likely to be well-rolled incense. A well-made incense will leave a pleasant but distant odor. It should not be aggressive and pungent.

Linen Closet

The linen closet is an underappreciated area in most homes. I know that is a pretty bold statement considering all the dusty and grimy places that can accumulate over time, but a wise woman once told me that and I found it to be true. The linen closet is the heart of the home. It's the place you go to ensure the family is cleaned properly. Here you store bath towels, washing clothes, sheet sets, pillowcases, extra blankets and so much more. Listen to this story and ode to the linen closet. Maybe then you will begin to understand why it deserves a bit more consideration.

"HAPPY PLACE"

"Hey, Mama Liz. I'm so happy you called."

"Well, hello dear. I hope you are feeling happy, happy today." Mama Liz responded with her usual cheer.

She always had a way of making me smile. Mama Liz wasn't my birth mother, but she raised me emotionally, mentally, and most of all spiritually since I was a teenager. Through puberty, graduation, college, marriage, and motherhood. Her calls would meet me right where I needed and today was no different.

"Well, I'm happy now that you called." I told her sincerely.

"What else are you doing to make yourself smile today," she asked.

"Just washing clothes and changing my sheets, the usual," I noted.

"Oh, lovely, linen day has always been one of my favorited days of the week." She replied. I could feel Mama Liz was beaming through the phone. It was almost like I time traveled with her for this story of the day. I had to listen intently. Her voice gently commanded undivided attention.

"When I was a little girl, I used to visit the linen closet often. Not to get a new towel or change my sheets, but because it was the one place in the house that always maintained order. The towels would be folded with the curves going in the same direction. Stacked from largest to smallest, same for the sheets and blankets. Along with linen, my mother and grandmother would always make sure we had a surplus of soap and bath tissue stocked there. I would take a peek to see how we were doing," she continued.

"What do I mean by that?" I wondered to myself and then found a window between her soft words to ask.

"When times were tight, the soap was low. We'd be down to one roll of toilet paper and I could tell that the air in the house was different. The linen closet had a way of gauging the financial stress level in our home."

"Well, you know I was born on the tail end of the Great Depression, February 17, 1940.

"Really?" I said quickly.

At that moment, even though we were over the phone, I could feel myself holding her hand. Her, walking with me down the halls and around the corners of her memories.

"I remember your birthday Mama Liz. Forty years before I made it to the planet." I said with a giggle.

"Yes dear, that was exactly during the depression era. I was lucky to only catch the end. Thank God the lack hasn't been as intense since. But I still go there. She graciously replied.

"Go where?" I said hanging on to her words with haste. My mind was still walking around her home in the '40s, imagining her as a sweet little girl.

"I go to the linen closet. I inspect it to see how my family's doing. Do we need more towels? Is it time to do laundry? Do we have enough soap, or do I need to order more? I still like to see things stacked and organized. Sometimes I just stop by when passing and straighten up anything out of order."

"What a beautiful memory," I uttered trying to condense the smile that was bursting from my time in her memory bank. I could smell the soap and see the stacks of towels and sheets. Everything is shelved with care and consideration.

She continued, "And when it is time to do our laundry, any old towels, ripped or worn, is no longer worthy to be geometrically aligned with the rest. It must go! When I fix our beds for the week any sheet that seems to need its own rest, must be departed with. If we couldn't afford to let it go, we would trim it or stitch it. Otherwise, tata!" Mama Liz chuckled knowing saying "tata" showed her seniority and placed a time stamp on herself.

"Maintaining the freshness of linen is an art. We should lay and embrace ourselves in the best-kept materials possible. It's not about the money. It's about the care," She continued.

"Sundays were linen days when I was a little girl, so I did the same when raising Yohanze. Bedding becomes stale and can make a whole room or home smell stale too."

I listened to every word while staring at my family's linen closet and realizing I had a few "tatas" to issue to our worn-out linen and things.

"Thank you so much for that story mama Liz. You always teach me something new. I realized through my time traveling experience with you today, that linen closets can be magical places. And even if you only have one set of sheets or one towel set for each member of your family, your linens and things should be intentionally selected and well-kept." I answered giving her a summary of her *class* that day.

"Yes, you are such a smart lady. I'm so proud of you." Mama Liz concluded.

She still loved me, even though my linen closet wasn't so magical at the moment and I was consistently imperfect. Her teachings came through with storytelling and I honored her loving delivery. Now I get to share a glimpse of her wisdom with you.

So, visit your linen closet today. *Cuay* it and be honored by its freshness. No matter if your linen "closet" is only one drawer right now. Whether it's a small cabinet or a full-length double door walk-in expression, visit it and respect it. And just like the heart is needed to circulate and maintain all the organs in your body, the linen closet is there to circulate and maintain the cleanliness and wellness of the home.

Excerpt from a heart-to-heart with my God-Mother Ms. Elizabeth "Mama Liz" Delores Daise (February 17, 1940 – January 13, 2019).

Car:

Vehicles are one of the hardest places to keep clean for many people. It's a location that you don't spend much time in and there usually isn't a trash can nearby, so things tend to pile up easily. Add the fact that many people eat at least one meal or snack in their car each day and you can imagine how crumbs and remnants of yesterday linger into today. Luckily, the CUAY steps we've covered apply perfectly to any space, including your car.

You can start by noticing the scent in your car. Follow it. If there is something being housed there that is causing an odor, start with removing it. Then go right into the 3 steps:

Sort and Share your Car

There are always things to sort in the car. Start with accumulated trash, various bags, receipts, and empty water bottles. If there is anything worth saving, separate it. Quickly decide if you want to use it later so you can find somewhere to house it. Give anything away that's worth saving but you don't anticipate yourself using.

Everything must have a home in the car. Umbrella in case of rain. Spare jacket for the chilly office, shades, make-up bag, lotion, hand sanitizer, pens, whatever you decide to keep. Decide where they belong and hold everyone who visits your car to the new standard.

Deep Cleaning your Car

Every now and then depending on your car care, you will need to get/give your car a deep clean. Whether that means signing up for a local car care program or having your children chip in as needed, get it done. Don't forget all those crevices where you dropped French fries last week or the residue left from that milkshake spill when you took that rough turn. Cars get grimy quickly and you have to be vigilant to keep up clean. Clean the inside door handles, dashboards, rugs, and seats before your car becomes a hot box for germs to multiply.

CUAY your Car All Day

Before you leave your car after each ride, take a look around to see what needs to go with you, ie. check the scene. Take everything out that does not have a home in your car and trash it or store it where it belongs. And most importantly: don't take car junk into the house to become home junk.

Application is Essential

We've covered many areas around your environment. If an area wasn't mentioned here, just apply the 3 steps to CUAYing and set your standard there as well. #CUAYlife

CHAPTER FOUR

CUAYING AROUND THE WORLD

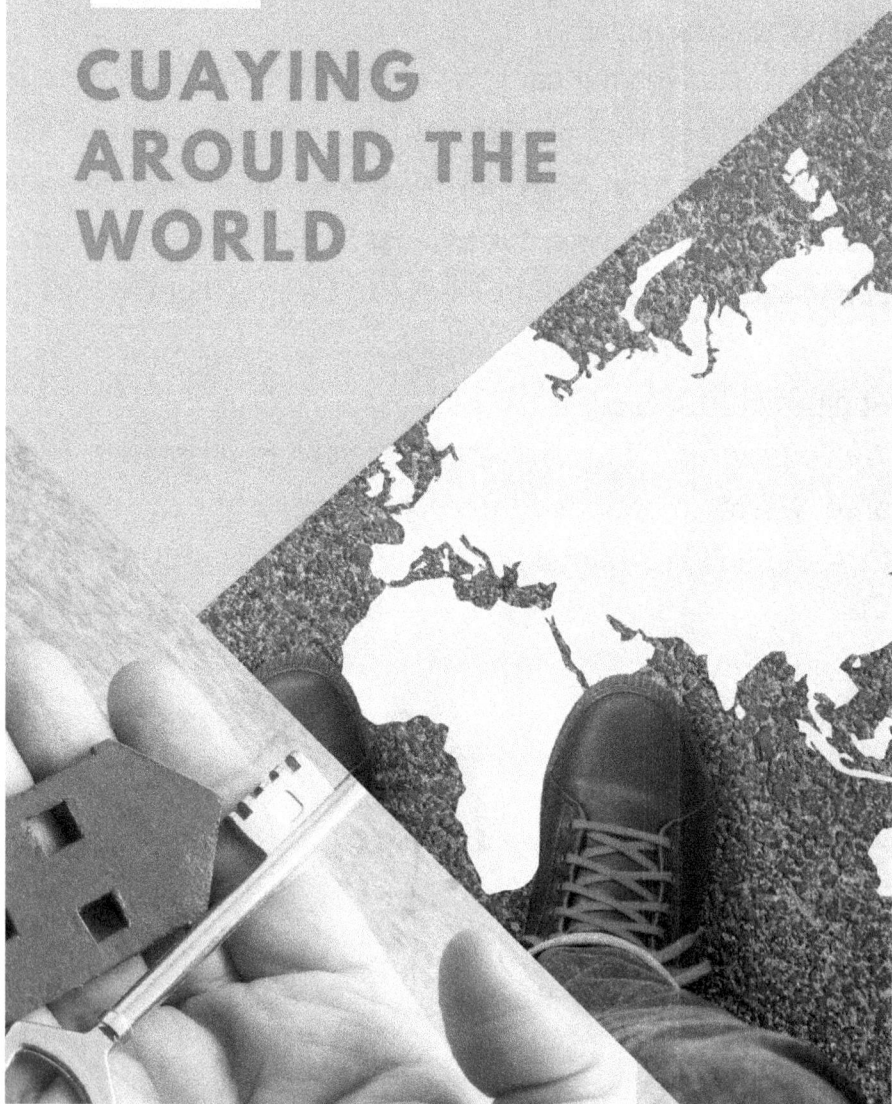

Chapter 4
CUAYing Around the World

By now, I'm sure you have officially added CUAY to your vocabulary. After reading, "How to CUAY," and taking the time to "Deep Clean" your area, it is important to take a step back and really get a clear understanding of why CUAYing is important. We'll look at CUAYing's importance on your Mental, Home, Community and eventually how it can make an impact around the world.

Mental

One of the greatest benefits of having a well-kept environment is its impact on our mental health. Before we can help anyone else or even think of impacting the world with organization, we have to establish that order within ourselves mentally. Going to sleep in a mess is one thing but waking up to it is a whole other problem. Mental health can be affected almost immediately when you look around to a space full of clutter, dirt, dust and, disorganization.

You should be able to close your eyes and mentally picture your home from corner to corner at any time. This is a good mental exercise to restore peace when you are frustrated or stressed away from home. You can go home in your mind.

If you visit home in your mind and still bump into that chair that sticks out around the corner in the front room, you need to move it. Reorganizing your space for a better flow makes a major difference in the room. Study the art of Feng Shui for tips or play with things around the house to test what feels right to you. Having an orderly living space helps relieve stress off of your mind so peace can live there instead.

There is a beautiful woman I know. Lovely mocha skin, dimples, especially coiled curls on her head, hourglass figure, and a gentle smile. She's an independent, hard-working woman within her community, eclectic, adventurous, and carries just the right amount of sassiness. When she steps out into the world her image is flawless. Light makeup but her presence can fill a room before she opens her mouth. Strangers would wonder, "Who is she?" But if they saw her home, they would be thinking, "How did SHE come from THIS?" Her appearance doesn't reflect her cleaning mentality.

She doesn't CUAY. She floats through her house ignoring all the clutter that she creates. Her outside demeanor doesn't match her housekeeping habits. It's easy to mask this bad habit when she first starts to date someone new by doing a one-time clean before inviting him for dinner. But when they see the real her, it becomes clear that there is an issue deep beneath her beauty. There's a blockage from her ability to maintain order in her environment.

If this sounds like you or someone you know and love, CUAYing is the perfect place to start. Circle back to the 3 steps, Sort and Share, Deep Clean, and CUAY All-Day. Making it a habit to check the scene before you leave will make all the difference.

Take time to build your organizational skills and hold yourself accountable to your goals. This will help you push past old mental brackets that kept you boxed in and can give you an opportunity to bring some order to your dome. Follow the 3-Step formula and don't give up.

Depression and Procrastination

Most people can see the benefit of cleaning up and recognize that having an environment that has order matters in life. Still, there are those who mentally cannot fully commit to getting started and staying consistent. This could be due to basic procrastination or living in a depressive state of mind.

Life happens and without having a productive outlet to release all the stresses that come your way, depression can build up and take over your mind. Even some medications can cause mental cloudiness that leads to depression. This is not a text to diagnose anyone's condition, only to acknowledge that mental blockages could be the reason you haven't been able to break loose of old habits of junkiness.

The first recommendation to shake off depression and get to CUAYing is to treat yourself like a plant. Sounds funny but it's true. Just like that house plant or that ever exploring weed in the backyard, humans need hydration, sunlight, and vital nutrients. Start there. Are you drinking at least half your body weight in ounces of water each day? Do you get at least 30 minutes of sunlight daily? Are you eating balanced, colorful foods, fruits, veggies, clean meat proteins, and rich grains?

The bridge between physical health and mental health merges at a place we experience without even thinking about it. Breath. Making time to breathe intentionally every day adds to your spiritual quiet time and will help to release a lot of trash from your mind and recenter you on your goals. So, breathe and be active to increase your breath capacity. Get active daily to get your blood flowing and increase your oxygen intake. If nothing else just walk.

Walk around the block. Walk the neighborhood. Walk across town. Walk to the park, to the store, with friends. Walk the dog. Walk with your family. Get out and move.

My Aunt Margaret was the walker in my family. She didn't drive until later in life. When I was growing up, we'd walk everywhere. One day it started raining when we were out on a walk. I started to run knowing we'd get there much faster. She said, "you'll just get wetter if you run." I was eleven and listened to her words like they were falling from the mouth of a sage. I never knew if she was right scientifically. But that walk in the rain taught me that rain showers can be medicine too.

If you already have physical wellness checked off your list and still feel like depression, procrastination or lack of vitality is an issue seek help. Talk to someone that can help. In many states now medicinal herb options are available to help balance your mind. Whatever you do, find a way to get out of that stuck place and flow again. No more scanning the room and holding your head down in disappointment to your current clutter. I'm excited to see you on the other side of the room. Looking at life through a CUAYed lens, where you have taken your life back and hold yourself accountable for the order in your dome and home.

Postpartum Depression*

I would be remised without mentioning that some forms of depression happens suddenly for mothers. After giving birth some mothers experience extreme mental distress before they time to notice it. Due to hormonal changes in the mother's body, emotions can be all over the place. Not only have you just experienced a miracle but you also now have a new addition to the family that is dependent on you to CUAY for them.

What if we all CUAYed for the new moms in our family and community? This is a needed government model for someone to work solely with new families in helping them to clean and stay well while their new baby is transitioning into the family. For most families, it will take a few months to get settled and create a new family routine, but it will happen.

That alone is a big transition, but mothers have to be mindful to take care of themselves primarily. If we as mothers are not well, the entire family suffers systemically. This is where family and community come in. Maternity leave is offered for the mother in many cases and she remains home to care for the new child and herself. Extended families have to step in to support and pay attention to the needs and changes that the expanded family is experiencing.

Home

Will everyone in your home see the value in CUAYing? Will they commit to lending a hand to keep your common areas presentable at all times? Hopefully. But it's likely that you'll have a rogue family member who is slow to get with the program. Some people have a hard time changing deep-seeded habits. You can read it to them, post it on the walls, sing it in a song, get loud, be sweet and get angry but they remain the same. Whether it is your spouse or your child, you play a role in their hygiene and cleaning behaviors. Sorry to tell you but you are a part of the problem.

It could be because you always clean up after them and they've never developed the independence to do it themselves. It is sad to say, but we easily enable our family members by not allowing them the opportunity to push past their comfort zones to do what's best for the family. What ends up happening is the natural cleaners can't stand the mess, so they take over the responsibility to keep things in order. It is a normal response but for many households, the lack of universal order causes major conflict. One of the goals of this book is to help mend those areas in families and open the door for communication and change to take place.

CUAYing for Others

If you have a young child in your house, no matter their age, you will have to gently phase them into CUAYing independently. It WILL take time. Start by making them responsible for one room at first. Or for smaller children, allow them to be responsible for a specific area: clearing the floor, putting their shoes away, sorting trash in the right area. Once they get that down, add on other tasks and take it day by day. But remember it is a learning process, which means you have to start releasing your expectations. While it likely won't meet your standards at first, over time they'll get it.

In our home, we have one main rule: *Chores BEFORE chill*! That's foundational. There is no chilling while there are still chores yet to be completed. Implement this rule in your home to jumpstart the accountability of chore completion for everyone. That means mom and dad too. Even if you've had the longest day and are ready to relax. If we left our home tidy in the morning, then we wouldn't be coming home to a mess. When it's clean, we can come home and unwind for a moment before we get to our evening responsibilities.

While you are in the CUAY learning curve and releasing the need to CUAY for that family member, you'll need lots of prayers. It is not an easy thing to do but I like to say, "Pray while you CUAY."

Pray While You CUAY

Cleaning and praying are connected. I'm sure you've heard the age-old saying, "Cleanliness is next to Godliness." It's true. All things under the sun are creations from the Most-High no matter what you call it. Ultimately, everything has its order. When things are out of order, they have a ripple effect on everything else and this pattern can be seen in our homes too.

As we make CUAYing a lifestyle, it is highly recommended that you add prayer to your practice. Positive thoughts, affirmations, words of gratitude, wants, needs, dreams, and more should be recited as you perform your tasks. This can be done aloud or intentionally in your head. There is no need in doing it with a bad attitude. It won't make things get cleaned faster, and it will simply spread negativity around your home, car, or workspace. Though CUAYing won't make your problems go away, prayer can soothe you in the meantime. CUAYing will give you one less thing to worry about because whether or not the problem is diminished, you'll have a peaceful place to rest your head.

Try praying while you CUAY and let that joy seep into every corner of your environment. Bless your home. Play some good music or motivational messages, dance your way to the trash can, fold those clothes with a smile. Give thanks that you have the ability to keep your area in order and the will to do it as well. It truly is a blessing to have a place of your own to maintain. Give thanks for that. Even if it's a room at a rooming house. Cater to it with joy and gratitude.

Cleanliness is next to Godliness because we can't even see clearly, listen completely or sense the presence of the Most High when we are bogged down with clutter, distractions, and mess. You'll be surprised how enjoyable praying while completing CUAY tasks becomes when you look up afterward and there's only order surrounding you.

CUAYing or Playing

There are those family members that have a hard time adjusting and then there are those who seem enthusiastic at first, but you'll notice they aren't even CUAYing, they're playing. There is a simple question to ask once you realize it. Just ask them, *"Are you CUAYing or PLAYing?"* If they are CUAYing, you should see some progress. Give them a timeframe to work with, where you will be expecting progress. Depending on the area, 15 minutes should be enough to see some growth and even some completion.

If you haven't been successful because the children or even adults always get distracted there's a reason. After observing the behavior patterns in your household, you'll generally find those having difficulty will need to work on one of the following three areas:

1. Items don't have a clearly defined HOME
2. The individual doesn't have a project that motivates them to CUAY quickly
3. There are some attention or discipline issues that have to be addressed

Find out which one of these issues needs to be addressed and confront it directly. Once you have done so you are able to move past that hurdle.

If you're wondering, can CUAYing be fun? Absolutely. But more so, it turns into a habit and becomes a part of who you are. CUAYing is a challenge. But you have to commit to it for it to begin to take root.

Community

A stroll in most towns- around various neighborhoods- would give you a glimpse of who tosses their trash in the wind. It is not to offend anyone, only to make a note that when we all take having a neat environment seriously and invest in our communities, the impact is immediately visible. When our family lived in an area where CUAYing didn't seem to be the norm, the kids always commented on the amount of trash in the streets. We took initiative and bought clamping tools for each of us to collect the trash ourselves when we walked.

Cleaning up our community became a new normal for us and it was a character-building exercise. We weren't just cleaning up after ourselves, we were helping take care of our entire community. People driving by would honk and shout, "Thank you", or "That's so nice." Our leadership and presence picking up trash made our community members more cognizant of what they left behind.

Start a meetup group if your community has similar needs. As your collective grows, maybe you can adopt a highway and commit to keeping one area kept by the hands of the neighbors who want to see their community in better condition. Remember to participate with joy, not bitterness or disgust. It can be a dirty job, but in many instances, the areas that are overlooked, trash-filled and unkept are not managed by the town or city. Write a letter to your elected officials about your neighborhood's needs to let them know that you care. We should be able to walk through our neighborhoods without stepping on trash regardless of how big the houses are or what side of town we're on.

If you toss trash out of your car window instead of holding on to it until you reach a trash can, do the world a favor- STOP IT. Keep a small grocery bag in the car or get small disposable rolled bags for random trash and drop it in the bin when you get home. We have to take responsibility for ourselves and CUAY all day, especially out in our communities. The children are watching.

Applying these practices everywhere we go will change the fabric of humanity. It will create a norm where cleaning up after yourself is expected. Where children are raised with a new word in their vocabulary that activates individual accountability. Where teenagers are growing towards becoming CUAY professionals before graduating high school.

By using and sharing the 3 steps here we can CUAY around the world with smiles on our faces and joy in our hearts.

"Power moves but is never moved. When man stands calm and serene, has good appetite, feels contented and happy when appearances are against him, he has reached mastery."
Florence Scovel Shinn, Your Word is Your Wand

CHAPTER FIVE

THE CLEANING OVERDOSE

CHAPTER 5:
The Cleaning Overdose

How do you define a passing grade? If your child brought home a 60% would you congratulate them on a job well done? Or would you expect them to do better? Some of us leave our homes at 60% cleaned habitually which means that nearly half of our surroundings are NOT cleaned and sanitized. Some may think this is hard to overcome because they have yet to make the necessary adaptations in everyday life.

Still, there is another side that has to be mentioned. Those who willfully commit to the process and seek to have their home, office, and car at 100% all the time. Beware of the CUAY overdose. The last thing I want to do is have someone go overboard. Take time as a family to decide on a CUAY percentage that is right for your home but 80% and up should be the goal. Maybe everything is clear and in its home place, but the floors need to be swept. Be okay with getting to that task when you can or assign it to someone's chore list to be completed sooner. But don't stress yourself to be at 100% all the time.

In a fresh hotel room, we marvel at the clear countertops, lack of clutter, clean sinks, and perfectly vacuumed floors among everything else. Yet, after we move in and stay for a day or so, it no longer looks picture perfect. We have to accept that it won't be at 100% again during our stay or at least not until the cleaning crew comes back through.

While tidying should be a daily task to avoid buildup, we have to be mindful our homes are going to look lived-in. It's okay to not have your house shoes side by side every time you get in the bed. Or that you tried to hang your housecoat and it fell overnight. Appreciate the little things that reflect the life growing there.

My grand-fathers wife, grandma Jonnie is a habitual CUAYer. I didn't understand it as a young person, but as an adult, I see that she's a woman of service. She enjoys serving others and has the energy to keep it moving. She can't stand things being out of order or in need of attention. When you visit her, she will do everything for you? That's not that uncommon for a hostess, especially when you have a new guest to your home. But for my grandmother, even when she visits you, she will most assuredly tend to your house during her stay. It would be with all due respect, but her energy keeps her moving, and rather than sitting on the couch talking about the news or complaining, she'll find her way to your broom and sweep or get that stubborn stain out of your countertop.

It is important to note that for some people having their home or environment on 100% isn't an overdose, it's their default. For my grandmother in particular it's her nature to CUAY and as long as she isn't stressing herself, disturbing others, or demanding them to do the same, it is a smooth experience. She's just an overachiever, not an overdoser.

Respect the CUAY overachiever personality type if you are lucky enough to have one in the family. They are actually seeking the kingdom right before your eyes. Buy them dinner more often or treat them to a spa day or pick up their favorite snacks for the weekend movie night. Make sure they know that you appreciate their efforts and impact on the family.

So, take a good look and identify the CUAY overachievers or CUAY overdosers in your family. The difference is: one is a healthy way to serve your household and the other is a nervous habit of not relaxing your mind or spirit which can be very unhealthy long term. Could you settle for 95% CUAY every now and then? Or will you worry yourself crazy about those drapes that need washing or the baseboards that need to be painted? Relax. Take time to enjoy the fruits of your labor.

Too much of anything can become a problem. Don't let CUAYing stress you. Set goals, delegate tasks to share the load, and understand that having a 100% clean home all the time may not be realistic for your family. Find your balance.

> "The Soul of the World is nourished by people's happiness." Paulo Coelho, The Alchemist

cuay first

CLEAN UP AFTER YOURSELF

CUAY

24/7

/'KWAY'/

Clean Up After Yourself

CHAPTER SIX

———

BODY AND HYGIENE

CHAPTER 6:
Body & Hygiene

When it comes to bodily hygiene*, the general rule is to bathe daily. While it sounds simple, there are adults that have never mastered this routine. People who don't practice adequate bodily hygiene could suffer from infections and body odor. No one wants to be the smelly person in class or at work. So, people often try to mask their odor with perfumes or cologne, but it is not sufficient. Careful bathing is necessary before applying any fragrance.

We will concentrate on the following essential areas of the body and hygiene: bathing, private areas, menstrual care, and intimate care. Stick with me through the menstruation section even if you don't experience it, it is vital that everyone has an idea of general care for both sexes. One day you may have a child, parent, or loved one to take care of and you will need this information to support your efforts.

Mastering our bodies and hygiene is essential for all humans as they develop into adulthood. Though some readers may be prepubescent or have yet to experience physical intimacy, this section is meant to be educational to supplement parental guidance for younger readers. This text is for educational purposes.

However, when it comes to body and hygiene, bathing is the primary concern and will be where we start. This lesson came to me when I was ten years old, still getting bathed by my grandmother...

"BOILING GOODNESS"

Grandma Gwen was her name. She'd raised seven "head of children" of her own and eventually ended up raising me too. But before she was my primary guardian, she was just Grandma. I used to stay the night at her house growing up and with over 20 first cousins in the mix, we all knew a stay at grandma's was a vacation from your parents' rules. You could count on eating good, watching anything you wanted on the TV in the back and there was even a chance for a trip to get ice cream when grandad was still alive. Grandma giving you a bath was the only drawback to spending the nights with her. Some of my cousins might have been approaching their teenage years when they had their last wash up with grandma. I distinctly remember being 10 years old the last time my grandmother washed me...

I was finishing my dinner when grandma called me for bath time. Though I was ecstatic to be enjoying the last

Italian baked chicken wing from her famous recipe, I dreaded what was to come.

I was double digits and washed my own self at home. My mama didn't bathe me anymore, so why didn't she tell grandma that I could handle it myself?

Well, maybe she's just telling me it's bath time and she won't be in there with me this time," I said out loud to myself in the kitchen.

Bath time at grandma's house wasn't a regular bath. It was like taking your skin to the cleaners for professional treatment. And afterward, every inch of skin from head to toe could squeak and tell its own story. Much more than the spa commercials I'd seen, grandma would scrub so hard you might end up a few shades lighter by the time she was through. So, I took extra-long that night to eat my chicken. But she didn't wait- I could hear the screech from the faucet as she began to draw my bath.

I wanted to screech too.

"No Grandma. Please don't wash me this time, I can do it myself" I pleaded in my head. But for some reason, I couldn't muster the courage to say it. The words were there, ready, but they wouldn't come out of my mouth.

I was near traumatized by this bathing experience. Not only was the scrubbing hard but the water was excessively hot too. I could barely sit in it. I guess the boiling was meant to prepare your body for the extra abrasive scouring. My heart was racing.

My pulse skyrocketed as I took my time to eat and put my plate away. Grandad was a quiet man, but I longed for just a few profound words from him to save me from the quickly approaching bath.

My grandma called to me again, "Go on in the room and take off those dirty clothes. I left your towel and washrag on the bed. I'll meet you in the bathroom."

Following directions was never an issue for me. But these directions, I did not agree with. Grandma Gwen was a sweet lady who spoke kindly with the kind of voice that sounded like a voicemail. But one thing she wasn't about was playing games. So, I knew I had to get moving. I'd seen my grandma get the switch for my cousins and brother and I didn't want to meet that same fate tonight.

The pink walls throughout the house reminded me of the medicine for upset and nervous stomachs like the one I was experiencing as I stripped down to my birthday suit that night. I wrapped the towel around myself and grabbed my washrag. Grandma's house was a shotgun two-bedroom home with a bathroom between the two rooms so there wasn't much distance between me and the boiling treatment. But that night, it felt like a mile. Each step was emphasized with the creaking of my feet meeting the old 1950s built floors. She was sitting on the toilet seat waiting for me when I reached the door.

"Come on child, I need to clean up that kitchen before I go to bed. You know I don't like leaving food on my stove." Grandma said as if I cared about her kitchen etiquette.

It smelled good in the bathroom, like flowers offered for forgiveness. The scent didn't seem to match the moment. I took a deep breath, hoping the words would come out that she could leave, and I had it from there. But I continued to move in silence as I put my towel on the shelf and dropped my washcloth into the tub. That was my way of testing the temperature. Did the blue cloth change colors from the heat of the water? Did it bubble up and boil? I could see the steam elevating from the bathwater, so it was as hot as expected.

"Get on in," Grandma said with a bit of haste in her voice at my passiveness.

"Yes ma'am," I said, praying my sweetness would make her take it easy on the scrubbing session.

Her bathtub had feet on it and there was no shower, so a bath was my only option. I reached my long, ten-year-old leg over the front of the tub to step in. It was hot at the first toe dip. But once the foot was in, the tingles would send a message to your leg sending a warning that it was next. I swirled that one foot in for a few moments before I swung the other foot in to join. I could feel my toes separating.

"Sit on down chile. What's taking you so long?" grandma murmured.

"It's hot Grandma."

"What, you want to take a cold bath?" "That don't even make no sense." She said as she turned the cold water on with a slow trickle.

After my feet were acclimated, I dropped to my knees. I wish the trickle of cold water had reached me by then, but the water still felt the same. A few more breaths and I was ready to sit down. I tried to swirl the cold water in with my hands but just as my cheeks hit the water, the heat set in. It was scorching! My body was tingling all over. Before I had a moment to get comfortable, Grandma came in with the washcloth, dunking it in the water and then raising it to drench my shoulders and back. I was feeling more and more like a soiled piece of clothing on an old washboard.

There was no time to waste, and grandma had a kitchen to clean. She grabbed the white bar soap and started with my face, erasing the history of the day. Then she proceeded to my front, arms and armpits. The armpits had to be her favorite spot because she spent a lot of time there dunking and scrubbing. Then she had me stand up to scrub the lower half of my body and lastly my toes.

Maybe it was the elevated body temperature or the deep skin exfoliation that amped me up, but I finally had the courage to speak up.

"Grandma, I know how to wash myself now, my mama taught me," I said softly.

"Oh, do you? Let me see," grandma replied.

So, I took the washcloth and did a full body wash all over again. She watched to see if I knew how to clean every part of me. I took my time, knowing my performance was under close examination.

When I was done, she gave me the side-eye and said, "You did pretty good, but if you ever smell sour walking around me, I'm going to have to start washing you again."

There was a knock at the door followed by, "Y'all hurry on up in there, I need to use the bathroom."

If only grandad had knocked a little sooner my scrubbing session could have been cut short. But it was all over, and I was excited at this point.

"I did it," I whispered to myself.

"What you say?" grandma asked, wondering if I was talking back to grandad.

I figured it might have been a little too soon to tell her how happy I was that she never had to wash me again, so I brushed it off, but it was a monumental occasion for me. I had finally graduated from getting washed by grandma. But she didn't trust me to clean her tub the way she liked, and I wasn't going to sign up for that chore too, so she sent me on my way back to the guest room to get ready for bed. I towel-dried, moisturized, and laid down to rest. But before I closed my eyes, I remember making a commitment to myself to always scrub so well that Grandma would never smell me. That's the only way I can be sure she wouldn't wash me again. Come to think of it, I got some good sleep that night. I guess my skin liked being boiled and squeaky clean after all.

BATHING

From my lessons on *Boiling Goodness* with my grandmother, I learned that a good full body scrub is essential to maintaining your human vessel. It wasn't until I became an adult that I realized the scrubbing my grandmother taught was actually called exfoliation. My aunt Alisha raised her children to do one hard wash and one soft scrub. This was a good way to proceed in case you missed a spot. Double duty bathing is a great habit for optimal hygiene. Exfoliating takes it a step further and activates the top layer of skin to remove the old, dead cells and uncover fresh, healthy skin. Using an exfoliating cloth regularly helps keep skin healthy but remember too much of anything can be bad.

Bath Soaps

Read it before you eat it. I know you're not really eating the soap, but your body is. So, what's in it? What's your body absorbing? Popular soaps with heavy fragrance and nostalgia of growing up at grandma's house typically contain chemicals like *sodium lauroyl isethionate, stearic acid, sodium tallowate or sodium palmitate, lauric acid, sodium stearate, cocamidopropyl betaine, sodium cocoate, fragrance, chloride, tetrasodium etidronate, titanium dioxide.* These types of chemicals and many more are not necessary to clean the body.

These chemicals have been known to aggravate the skin and cause build up in the bodies, liver, kidneys, or reproductive organs. The build-up of those toxins in your body can have harmful effects on the body and have in some instances been linked to cancer-causing agents. If interested, continue your research on skin-care products and the growing movement back to natural bathing options.

It's time that we seek better products for our skin to drink and be nourished from, ingredients like essential oils, shea butter, palm kernel, goat or oat milk, mint, olive oil, lemongrass, mango, papaya, green tea, or chai. Look for simple ingredients that you can pronounce and understand. Check the ingredients of the soap in your bathroom. If it doesn't pass the clean ingredient test, toss it.

Scrubbing vs Exfoliating

If you've seen body wash commercials these days, you'd think all you have to do is squirt it in your hand and rub it in. But cleansing your body is more than that. You have to scrub it, otherwise, you are only deodorizing yourself, not really bathing. Natural fiber cloths are perfect to lather up and scrub away the layer of dead skin, oil, dirt, and bacteria that has accumulated throughout the day. You may not be able to see it with your eyes but take a look at the bathtub after a thorough* bath or shower, you'll likely see dirt lingering.

One of my teachers, Dr. Jewel Pookrum recommends exfoliation for anyone over the age of two. By then, your baby soft skin is in the past and external exposure requires that you wash off the old to make way for the new. Run a few trials for exfoliating products and find which gives you the best results. I fell in love with an exfoliating cloth that I used religiously, my skin loved it and I felt more hydrated after adding this cloth to my bath time. Then I started noticing that my skin was breaking out in small, bumpy patches, most notably on my stomach and thighs. The only difference I could note was regular use of the cloth and once I stopped, the rash subsided. I was over exfoliating and being abrasive with my skin.

Use exfoliation on your face and body weekly but pay attention to your results and avoid causing irritation. Anytime you notice something out of the ordinary with your skin, it is important that you pay attention to any recent changes in your skincare routines.

Crevices

After you've mastered cleaning your skin, it's time to get to the hot spots- the crevices. Just like around our home, there are crevices on our bodies that must be tended to. Think of anywhere there is a fold on your body, that area may not get adequate attention. If you just stand under the water and slide a bar of soap across your body, these crevices have been neglected for quite some time. We are going to review the main hot spots on all bodies, then proceed to more intimate crevices. When you begin to CUAY your body you want to start at the top.

UPPER BODY

There is something about allowing water to wash over your head that is quite rejuvenating. However, melanated people with coily hair have to make sure we are properly moisturizing our hair when it is wet a lot, in order to keep it healthy. For CUAYing body purpose, we will assume this is a hair rinse day and you are showering from head to toe. An amazing time to CUAY and pray is in the shower or bath. Get your head cleansing in by rinsing your head thoroughly. No soap is needed on your face unless you have a skin regime that you implement in the shower. Proceed. Otherwise, warm water will suffice.

GUIDE TO CUAYING YOUR HEAD

Face

Warm cloth to cover your **face** and breathe

<u>Mouth and teeth</u>:

Practicing good oral hygiene is one of my favorite parts of my personal CUAY routine. While there is an ongoing debate on which toothpaste reigns supreme, there are ways you can boost your oral health.

<u>Baking soda</u>∗: use a teaspoon of baking soda on your wet toothbrush to gently exfoliate* your teeth and gum line. Because it is naturally a base, it provides alkalinity and helps to balance the pH of your mouth, preventing a buildup of bacteria that thrive in acidic conditions. Again, too much of anything isn't good so remember that baking soda is for brushing and not eating, as it is sodium based.

<u>Activated Charcoal</u>∗: It's black, powdery and used for multiple purposes to sanitize, and extract toxins from the body. It can be found in a paste form as well and used to whiten teeth naturally. Just rinse well after use.

<u>Unrefined Virgin Coconut Oil Pulling</u>:

This is not to replace actually brushing your teeth but gargling with coconut oil sanitizes your mouth and strengthens facial muscles that keep your face looking youthful. Remember to spit it out when you're done, don't swallow or else you'll ingest all the toxins your body just pulled out of your mouth.

Eyes

Be gentle around your eyes as you are removing eye boogers or makeup. The skin right below your eyes is most sensitive and you should limit the abrasion in that area as much as possible. Damage to the skin around the eyes can lead to the appearance of dark circles or water retention in that area. But mostly dehydration causes issues in this area. So, stay hydrated and keep this area moisturized.

Ears

Use a damp cloth to cleanse the curves and crevices of your ear. You don't have to go deep but cleaning your ears when you bathe will minimize the need for cotton swabs or dewaxing. This is another crevice that gets missed often. Odors will arise around your ears when they are not cleaned all the way around the back. Dirt and grease accumulate here, and you should scrub it daily to maintain. Remember to always clean around earring holes as well.

Nose

Inside our noses can be dusty. It's our filter just like you clean the filter in your home periodically you have to clean the filter of your body more often. Daily. For nose ring wearers, clean around there for optimal freshness.

Back of the neck

I've seen the back of some necks as a teacher, that let me know their parents didn't teach them to bathe properly. When was the last time you examined the back of your neck? Take a mirror to check. If it's looking greasy, dirty, or darker than your face, it's likely because you don't wash that part of your body as often. Other reasons can be associated with health disparities such as diabetes. Either way, the back of the neck cannot be neglected. Do a scratch test to see if you have dirt on yours right quick. Exfoliate that and scrub it daily.

Front of the neck

CUAY your neck by always wiping up. Grandma Gwen always said work against gravity when dealing with your face and neck will keep your neck young. Wipe up, not down.

Facials

Facials should be free. It's an open appreciation of your face. Everyone deserves that. Invite a friend over for a facial meet up. The nice part about doing facials with friends is the talking is limited. Everyone's face is tightly covered in their mask of choice. Play some music or an inspirational message and get your facial on.

There are loads of facial and mask products on the market. Here are a few simple ones that do the trick.

Clay Masks:

Clay masks are great for clearing blemishes and evening out your skin tone. They are pretty inexpensive to find as well. The clay mask takes a while to remove because it is thick. So, avoid putting this mask under your eyes directly. You don't want to be rubbing it too hard when it's time to come off.

Sea Moss Masks:

Sea Moss* masks are ideal for rejuvenating your skin. Sea Moss has 92 of the 102 minerals our body needs. It is great to take it internally. But applying it directly to your skin softens your skin tremendously. Because this mask is so nutrient-rich and nonabrasive, it is okay to use it under your eyes if you like. It can even help reduce the dark circles.

Baking Soda* Mask:

One of my favorite masks is the baking soda mask. It is an exfoliate that gently tightens and closes the pores on your face. This is one that I would not put under my eyes in the sensitive area. Remember to exfoliate as needed or at least twice a month.

<u>Removing facial masks</u>:

To remove a mask from your face, start with a hot/warm towel to your comfort level. Lay it on your face where it is damp, but not dripping all over the place. Depending on the thickness of your mask you may need to do this a few times to moisturize the mask before you begin to remove it. Take your time. It is a process, not a race. Facial times should be relaxing where you settle your mind and enjoy.

YOUR ARMS AND TORSO

Armpits

Individuals will decide if they prefer hair under your arms or not. But the overall method to keep your armpits clean and fresh is simple. Scrub thoroughly and exfoliate as needed. You have loads of veins and arteries in this area. It's a circulatory system highway. There are also hormonal glands in this area, so dirt and sweat may accumulate here. Use your favorite natural oil or cream to shave with CLEAN blades and you will be good to go.

Entire Back

This is a test of flexibility. If you are not able to reach your entire back for scrubbing please get a bathing tool to assist you. Otherwise using a soapy cloth reach around to scrub your upper, lower, and side parts of your back. Ask a family member for help if available. Getting your back scrubbed feels like the ultimate grooming. Enjoy and make this a necessity to CUAYing your body daily.

Elbows

Often overlooked, elbows go out into the world looking unloved and unkept. Scrub and exfoliate your elbows daily for proper care. Show the elbows some love with extra moisturization.

Belly Button

Inny or outie belly buttons can get grimy. Soap up your belly button daily. Test your belly button cleaning skills by rubbing your finger in there prior to bathing. They can carry an odor when dirt builds up. Any areas within the belly button that tend to be missed during daily bathing can also be cleaned ever so often with a cotton swab and alcohol.

Arm crevice

It's the other side of the elbow. The infamous sweat spot of the arm. No one wants to raise their hands or open their arms for a hug and reveal last week's dirt in the crease. Keep this crease clean by scrubbing it daily.

Nipples

Nipples are alive. Even if they aren't being used to feed anyone. They need to be scrubbed and even exfoliated in your CUAYing the body rituals too. It's always good to do a weekly check-in with your breast when you are showering too. Feel around for anything abnormal that you may feel or any pain. Pay attention to your body. It is your compass.

Hands

Not many people wash their hands in the shower or bath. But we should. Our hands should be scrubbed and exfoliated as needed as well. Manicures are magical. Fingers need attention too.

Fingernails

If you are walking around with dirty fingernails this tells me, you are likely not washing properly. Even if you work in a garden, automotive care, or are a professional booger picker, you should be cleaning your nails or risk transmitting germs from your hands to your mouth and family. CUAY your nails and keep an eye out for nail dirt. It's honestly not a good look.

LOWER BODY

Gluteal Muscles

These are the three muscles that make up your butt. The Gluteus Maximus is the largest muscle of the three and on your body. It is responsible for holding the body upright, running, climbing, and walking. But it is often overlooked when it comes to bathing. CUAYing your glutes is easy. Just scrub them thoroughly and exfoliate as needed. Be sure to scrub the lower crease of the glutes as dirt can settle there.

Anus

When we say butt, most people think of the ending of our digestive tract, the anus. This area of the body is PRIME when it comes to CUAYing and can easily become an odor bomb when not cleaned appropriately. The secret to keeping a clean anus is primal. Smell it! Of course, our bodies are not naturally flexible enough to reach it with our noses, so we have to use our wiping skills to aid us.

To CUAY your anus use a soapy lathered cloth and wipe from front to back. This means that your hand should always be moving towards your back. Not the other way around. This way you are not wiping bowels into your private area. Continue to clean your anus until you no longer smell bowels on your washcloth. Be sure to rinse and or fold your cloth in-between anal washes so that a fresh part of the cloth is used each time. You may need to rinse completely to soap and lather up to get the freshest clean.

Digestive tract

A healthy and fairly clean digestive tract is passing at least one bowel movement each day. If not, you are experiencing some form of constipation. This could be due to dehydration or not eating enough fiber-rich foods. Plan a smooth move day for an intestinal detox or consult your wellness provider for support on regulating your bowels. A CUAYed digestive tract is flowing and not stopped up with constipation.

One way to keep your digestive system cleaned out is to incorporate seasonal times of the year to detox your body. By reducing your processed food intake or fasting completely you give your system an opportunity to rest. This can be done during four key points of the year. Remember those times to clean your closet, you can use those times to clean your internal body as well. Winter to spring on March 22nd Spring Equinox or Fall Equinox on September 22nd. At both times of the year, the day and night are equal. Then during Spring to Summer on June 22nd Solstice is the longest day of the year and or the Winter Solstice on December 22nd is the longest night of the year.

Seasonal fasting is an ancient practice of fine tuning the body and can be found throughout history in many different cultures.

Private areas

Scrubbing, washing with gentle soaps, rinsing well, drying thoroughly, and exfoliating as needed is the basics for all private areas of the body.

Male Genitals

The male genitals consist of a penis/rod and a scrotum* with two testes. They hang on the outside and simple scrubbing and occasional exfoliation will usually suffice when it comes to CUAYing. The scrotum hangs under the penis* away from the body. The seed of a mature male is made and housed in the scrotum. It hangs away from the body because the temperature of the body is too hot for the process to happen naturally. So super-hot baths or sometimes showers can cause reproductive stress and direct contact to extreme heat should be avoided.

The scrotum should be handled with care during CUAYing or any other practices as it is an active organ. Scrub the scrotum by starting at the base of the penis and around both testes housed there. Under the scrotum can become sour and odorous if not CUAYed intentionally. There is a space between the scrotum and the anus called the perineum that should also be included in your scrubbing ritual.

Due to social indoctrination, some male genitals have been cut at birth or puberty called circumcision*.

Cut penis

A cut or circumcised penis has had four parts of the organ cut off. The Dartos Muscle* was at the very tip, the Ridged Band* is behind it, the Frenulum* which is usually extremely sensitive and found behind the glands and also part of the *outer skin* has been removed. Due to this surgical procedure, you should be very careful when CUAYing the penis. The glands/head of the penis, in most cases, should not need exfoliation. But the entire penis needs to be scrubbed as well as the gland/head. If not maintained well, a cut penis head can become calloused or calcified and lose sensation. So CUAYing it and wearing soft fabric clothing, can help the gland stay as supple as possible, considering it is not naturally covered.

Intact penis

An intact penis evolves over time from birth to puberty to manhood and should also be CUAYed with care. An uncircumcised/intact penis at birth has the Dartos Muscle attached to the gland. With maturity, the foreskin* naturally releases

the attachment to the gland and pulls back so the head/gland can be fully exposed. Intact penises have been known to have more sensation in the glands/head of the penis because of its foreskin protection from the elements of life day-to-day. When it comes to CUAYing, we DON'T have to retract the skin until it happens naturally. At that point, you want to CUAY the fully covered penis and retract to clean the glands. It is VITAL that you rinse well so no soap is left behind and dry thoroughly.

Female Genitals

The female genitals are encased inside vaginal lips called the labia* majora and the labia minora. At the top of the female genitals is a vital organ called the clitoris*. You can think of it as an under-development penis. Just add testosterone and the fetus changes to be a boy in the mother's womb instead of a girl. But part of the clitoris that is visible is only a button to the full organ that is beneath the skin. The clitoris is sensitive and should be handled with care and intention. The vagina is the most popular part of the female genitals in that it is the location of intimacy and birth in mature women.

To CUAY the female genitals you need to understand that the crevices matter. Wiping when you use the bathroom is a simple swipe front to back until dry. This means you are pushing the toilet paper from the front near your lower stomach back towards your anus and dropping it in the toilet. DO NOT DOUBLE WIPE with the same side of the toilet paper. You are inviting bacteria into your sacred space and it will lead to systemic odor-causing infections.

But to thoroughly CUAY the female genitals when bathing, you have to get between the crevices of the labia and clitoris. Again, be sure to use a gentle cleanser or freshwater, scrub gently between all the crevices, rinse extremely well and dry thoroughly when you are done. There is also the *perineum* between the *vagina* and the *anus* that must be CUAYed as well. It is the point of skin between the two areas.

The *vagina* is all internal, so when it comes to CUAYing there, we have to be strategic. Douching is a well-known method that has been used to cleanse the vagina by flushing it out with a gentle cleanser. It's a very sensitive area, so proceed with caution and be aware of your body. The vagina actually has a built-in CUAYing system during menstruation and we will get to that in a few. However, there are ancient techniques of *steaming your vagina* using specific herbs such as, oregano, chamomile, basil, mugwort, wormwood, and calendula among others, that can help with CUAYing internally. This is a practice that can be strategically done at home or with a steaming practitioner.

If you would like to steam to CUAY your vaginal area at home, invest in a steaming seat to make the process easier. I recommend **@LunaRainBotanicals** they have beautifully hand-crafted wooden steaming seats that will last a lifetime. All you have to do is purchase the steaming herbs and a 5-gallon bucket. Then prepare your water, add the herbs and relax.

Cut Female Genitals

Around the globe, there are still some women that are subject to female circumcision. It is not as common in America to date. However, it is important to consider. There are three different types of female circumcision cuts. (Clitoridectomy*, Excision*, or the Infibulation*). See CUAY vocabulary for details. The CUAYing guide for circumcised women is the same as above. Gentle products to cleanse with, scrubbing, rinsing well, and drying thoroughly. Be sure that you moisturize your genital area. The cutting can change the texture of the skin there and chaffing and discomfort may happen. Embrace what you have and keep it CUAYed.

Genital Shaving/Waxing & CUAYing

Shaving genitals is foreign to some people. They just leave them as they come. But many adults, young and old choose to cut or trim their genital hair for looks or convenience. Shaving can sometimes lead to bumps, which is a reaction to open and inflamed pores or clogged hair follicles. Waxing oftentimes means you have to have someone else to complete the task for you. Either way make sure you dry the area well after bathing. Use a toner or *astringent* after removing the hair, lightly moisturize the area, or use an antiseptic oil or spray for best results everywhere especially in private areas.

CUAYING LOWER EXTREMITIES

Thighs and Legs

To CUAY your thighs and legs follow the format for your skin. Scrub daily with gentle cleansing soap and exfoliate as needed.

Knees

CUAYing the knees takes a little more effort. As children mature, we should be mindful of their time on their knees. My mother always made it a point to keep me off my knees growing up. She would say, "You gonna make your knees black doing that." After becoming a mother, myself, I saw the difference. I was adamant about telling my daughter that wisdom and she listened. My son listened too, however, his multiple scrapes and bruises made his knees a lot rougher over time. If you have warrior's knees and need a reset, try exfoliating them more often than you would the rest of your lower extremities. The knees, like the elbows, will harden over harsh exposure. Scrub them, exfoliate them and keep them properly moisturized for best results. But if you want to maintain your regular skin tone on your knees, stay off of them unless they're cushioned appropriately.

Feet

One place that has a connection to every part of your body is your feet. Your feet tell a story about your past and if maintained, play a major role in your wellness moving into your future. When bathing always take a moment to clean between your toes. It's not only good to keep your feet fresh, but it also helps to stretch your toes out when they are usually hard at work balancing your body. Keep your feet loved and moisturized.

Heels

The heels of your feet are often overlooked, and they can be left crusty and unkept. Unless you are getting a pedicure every few days you will notice that skin builds up on your heels and the bottom of your feet quickly. Invest in a pumice rock or foot file to exfoliate your feet daily in-between professional or private pedicures. Keep your toenails trimmed to avoid ingrown toenails and proper shoe fit.

Moisturizing

To finalize our journey in CUAY Body and Hygiene, we have to cover moisturization. No matter what climate you live in moisturizing is crucial to maintaining healthy skin. Be sure that you read the ingredients of anything you are putting on your skin. Remember that your skin is the largest organ of the body. Whatever you put on it, it is literally drinking it up.

One of my favorite things to use to moisturize my skin is raw or whipped shea butter. It's smoothing and it lasts all day without leaving my skin feeling heavy. It is greasy at first though and some people prefer a lighter moisturization. Check out **@H2OilCompany**. It is a specially hydrated mist that you can spray on to your body from head to toe and rub in with ease. It's also great to use after a nice facial or nightly routine, to rub into the sensitive spots on your face, neck, and under the eyes. Another basic oil to use is unrefined coconut oil.

The joy of moisturizing is pure self-care. Massage your skin with a nutrient-rich oil, or cream-based moisturizer daily.

Take your time. Tell your knees thank you while you're there. Your glutes and hands, ankles and feet, breasts or nipples, between the toes and between the shoulders. Thank your body. Try to make it a habit every time you moisturize. Appreciate you. CUAY moisture.

Minimizing to the MAX

There are times when a garden tub isn't available for you to wade in. No shower head to sprinkle you or a clean place to sit to CUAY your body and hygiene. In this case, you must be able to minimize to the max. If all you have is one bucket, large bowel, or sink that can be used. First, clean it to the best of your ability. Using the warmest water available and a cloth, follow the CUAY skills and refresh your temple. You can get every crevice and hotspot of your body with a gallon of water or less. If there is a will to improve your body and hygiene by keeping it clean, a way will be made.

Bottom line

We could chat about CUAYing the body effectively forever. There is so much to share, research, and respect about our bodies. I am so grateful to have a history of loved ones in my life that taught me to CUAY my body for optimal hygiene. I know grown women that still don't know how to wipe their behinds properly. And men whose women say they don't wash their genitals thoroughly, so they always carry an odor. The objective of this section is to share details that will help readers grow in their hygiene and arise more knowledgeable and fragrant human. One who CUAYs effectively.

Find the right soap for your family. Teach them to lather up and scrub their entire bodies twice at each session and exfoliate as needed. Remember that hot water is useful to the cleansing process to take it as hot as you can stand it for optimal "boiling goodness." Keep your body CUAYed up. It's your temple and greatest gift. Take care of it and teach those around you to take care of theirs as well.

USING PUBLIC RESTROOMS

Honestly, a public restroom is my last resort. If I'm in there, it is because I'm too far away from a more comfortable or safe restroom. On the other hand, I don't recommend holding your bowels or bladder for extended periods either. Learning to CUAY in Public Bathrooms is essential for public health and common respect.

Toilet seats

Surprisingly, toilet seats are cleaner than handrails along stairs. Raise your hand if you used a handrail today, now go wash them. Still, a public toilet seat is not somewhere I want to rest my precious body. So, it is vital that you teach your daughters to hover over the toilet to urinate at an early age. Needless to say, we haven't mastered how to truly hover just yet. We can just call it squatting to pee for now.

Until a child is taller than the toilet seat to *hover* alone, an adult will have to hold them. Still, if no one is there you surely don't want your child climbing up on the toilet, holding onto the seat that multiple bodies have sat on in the nude, without some precautions. We have to teach them.

- CUAY before you stay

Once entering a stall, see if the last person CUAYed. Did they leave anything behind in the toilet? Did they flush? Is the seat or floor wet? If it's too much work to CUAY that place to your standards, walk away. Remember, you're on a mission to relieve yourself. It's urgent!

- To sit or not to sit

Do you have to do a number one or a number two? Are you squat certified? Can you hold your weight long enough to handle your business? Depending on those questions you decide if you are good with squatting it out for this restroom visit, or if you need to sit.

- Sitting

In preparation to sit down to handle your business, you need to make sure the seat is dry. You can test this out by leaning different angles while looking at the toilet seat. If it is dry, you are clear to go to phase two. Otherwise, you need to prepare for that phase first. To prepare, gather a wad of toilet paper and wipe off the toilet seat. This mission can go wrong quickly. If you don't use enough toilet paper and someone else's urine seeps through to wet your fingers, hit the reset and go wash your hands before continuing. Use as much toilet paper as you need. Not to waste. I always like to have a little paper in the toilet already before using it. Once I am seated, it helps with reducing the splashes.

- Layer it

Now that you are familiar with the toilet paper and realize you need to sit. Take sheets off the roll about the length of each side of the toilet seat. Lay down along the seat, not across the seat. This means there is no toilet paper covering the center of the toilet. You should not have to rip a hole to use it. You are laying paper across the seat, in 2-4 layers anytime seat protectors are not available.

Flushes

If you are making a bowel movement, boo-boo, number two, deuce, or whatever you call it, remember to flush often. This is where you will likely get splashed. Try to think it's clean water and not toilet germs. If it bothers you too much, just stand a bit while your flush. But do the people coming to wash their hands before lunch a favor by not having to smell your dinner last night.

Flush often until you are done. Using about a hand's length of toilet paper position yourself to flush the toilet. If standing, it is highly recommended that you practice balancing on one leg to flush. This is a yoga move that translates to real life. The core balancing needed here should be our human goals of maintaining our health and flexibility of our bodies.

Seat up or down

If a squat will do or you're standing anyway, you might as well leave the seat up when urinating in public bathrooms. Either way, you are going to have to clean the rim, or the seat when you're done. When you're squatting or standing remember to shake it when you're done! Ladies, a little twerk over the toilet after peeing will limit the number of wipes and toilet paper needed to dry off. While bracing yourself on your legs or in a full squat, bounce it a couple of times. Fellas need to shake too and even dab their penis/rods after urinating with a small amount of toilet paper.

Wiping (Private Care)

The goal is to dry yourself and not to leave any toilet paper behind after wiping. Carrying around the old, soiled paper in your private areas can get stinky. Wipe dry and proceed. Ladies remember you are always wiping front to back. That's from belly button to back area and no double wipes. Once you reach the anus drop the toilet paper and try again. If you cannot reach that far, pushing the toilet paper from front to back you can reach around the back and pull the toilet paper from the front to the back. It will always be front to back. Either pulling front to back or pushing front to back. Your preference is your choice.

After a bowel movement, you will have to wipe extra. Ideally, it is always good to wipe with something wet when you are looking to clean your anus effectively. That's when available. Be prepared for a spit clean if needed. A clean anus after a bowel movement means the toilet paper has no signs of fecal matter after your last wipe. In this case, you can be pretty comfortable pulling up your underwear without having streaks of fecal matter in there later. If you are prone to have lines in your underwear, it is because you are not wiping effectively after using the bathroom. If you can see the lines just trust the odor can be present as well. Wipe front to back until it is clean. And follow up with a gentle spit clean if needed. Hopefully, you CUAY your mouth and it's optimal to complete this mission. If you are home or close to the sink you can always wet the tissue with some water for the same effect. Or bathe.

Again, when you are done using the bathroom from standing or squatting, you will still need to wipe off any wetness before you leave it behind. It happens nearly every time. Dribbles happen, even on the floor. If you dribbled there, get your wad of toilet paper and CUAY.

Washing hands

Be creative when leaving the stall. You can use your elbow, toilet paper, shopping bag, or whatever to open the door of the restroom stall. Once you reach the sink area. Scan the scene. Where's the soap? Is the paper towel dispenser manual or electric? Is the sink area wet where it could get on your pants, hands, or arms. CUAY. Get a few paper towels and do wipe down the countertop in your area. If this is not needed simply wash your hands. If the soap dispenser or water faucet is manual you need to use the back of your hand instead of your regular grasp. This will reduce the amount of skin to skin contact with the public facilities.

Wash your hands thoroughly using soap and warm water for 30 seconds. You should be leaving the bathroom better than you found it in some way. So, use those thirty seconds to see what you need to CUAY before you leave. A quick sink wipe after you've dried your hands is good. Or wipe that stained soap out of the sink from the last person. If needed use a paper towel to turn off the water. NEVER use your clean hand to turn off the water. That's even at home, but especially in a public restroom. And finally, in regard to washing hands in public locations, be okay with air drying your hands. It happens and you'll live.

Not all public restrooms are dirty. Some are immaculate. Of course, those well-maintained restrooms have high rotation maintenance staff to keep them clean. You can do your part of helping a restroom that you frequent stay maintained by CUAYing every time you go and always leaving it better than you found it.

Menstruation

The onset of menstruation is a sacred time and transition in a young woman's life. Being a fifth-grade teacher, I have witnessed a lot of young girls move into menstruation without proper guidance. I did my best as their teacher to make it special for them but CUAYing is a culture, not just a thought. To look at menstruation through the CUAYing lens is to see that menstruation is really the body doing just that. Cleaning up after itself.

Once a month for most women, but it can be twice a month, an egg is released from the ovaries and heads to the uterus awaiting the perfect seed and the perfect timing to create a human. If that doesn't happen the body will begin to CUAY. It no longer needs the thick lining in the uterus to house a growing embryo. So, the unfertilized egg and the nutrient rich lining of the uterus sheds. It is actually not the vagina bleeding but the uterus which opens into the vagina. The vagina is simply the canal it flows through.

Again, the human body is amazing. Once the cycle begins it is up to the woman to decide how she will handle the blood of peace that will flow. Does she want to catch her cycle on pads that are then rolled up and tossed away. Or maybe she wants to soak it up like an internal sponge using a tampon. Cup options are now available where a silicone cup is inserted to catch the cycle before it exits the vagina.

Humans haven't explored all of the menstrual blood's potentialities. But at least it is coming to the surface that there are stem cells present there and it might not be a waste of the body after all. I implore you to inquire further if the topic interests you. The cycle of a woman is very interesting. We call it a cycle because it doesn't stop like a period- until menopause that is.

Disposing of Your Sanitary Options

Before you go to change your sanitary option... ALWAYS WASH YOUR HANDS.

Pads

Most women use pads during their cycle. To apply it you simply remove the adhesive backing and attach it to the inside of your underwear. Wrap the adhesive wings around if applicable and carry on. You have to be mindful of your cycle flow and how heavy your days go. Make sure the pad you select covers the full curve of your genital area. From your pubic bone back passed your anus. If not, you will likely have leaks that happen to the front or the back of the pad. Keep in mind that the flow can leak differently depending on how the pad is positioned.

After no more than 4 hours it is recommended that you refresh your pad or sanitary napkin. To do so, simply remove the pad from your underwear. Fold it in half and then roll it up. Use the plastic cover for your new pad to wrap your old one or some toilet paper. When you are done. It is a tightly rolled up bun that can be easily tossed in the trash. Pads are never to be flushed. They will clog up the plumbing.

Tampons

With freshly cleaned hands tampons are vaginally inserted cotton that absorbs your cycle and is removed by pulling the attached string. They are easy to insert as long as you have the right size. For safety purposes, you may want to start off using regulars to see if they are sufficient before you move on to supers. You don't want to be wearing a tampon for extended periods that are not absorbing. Such practices can lead to Toxic Shock Syndrome, which can be a huge health risk.

Most product guides say Tampons can be used for up to 8 hours. I suggest 4 to 6 at the max. Using the bathroom with a tampon takes some strategic technique for success. If you have to pee while you have a tampon inserted, you do not have to remove it. Simply use your freshly cleaned hands to grab the string and place it to the side of your labia in the crevice next to your inner thigh. If you forget and pee with the string hanging it will be wet. I suggest hitting the reset and removing and replacing that tampon if possible. Otherwise, you can attempt to dry the string with toilet paper. But for hygiene purposes, know that it won't dry all the way. And you will have a moist string hanging until you replace it.

Please note if you have to make a bowel movement, it is best to do so without a tampon inserted. The tampon can obstruct your lower bowel passage or even be pushed out during your bowel movement. In an urgent moment where you don't have a backup tampon and have to empty your bowels, you can try to tuck the string and go for it. But it is recommended that you remove any possible obstruction beforehand when possible.

Remember to talk to your teenagers or remind yourself before you start using tampons to make sure you are responsible enough and understand the pros and cons. Pros are you can wear it longer than pads, the odor is less from airborne blood drying in your undies. And you are able to swim and be more active with a tampon.

When I was 13 my mother found that I had used one of her tampons to go to a dance party. I didn't want to sweat and have that pad on. I thought I was being responsible, but she was offended because in her mind this meant that I wasn't a virgin. I was. She had never discussed using tampons with me and had no idea of my research and education on using them. But to her, it was a sign that I had been having sex. Parents, please note, wearing a tampon does not equate to losing your virginity. It is a false ideology and misconception that caused such confusion in my childhood. Give your teenage daughters the option ONLY after you feel they can handle the maturity of it. TSS is real.

As a mother, I demonstrated using a tampon to my daughter during her second year of having a menstrual cycle. Later when she was visiting her father for the summer and wanted to swim, she took it upon herself to get tampons. She felt empowered having that option. I was in shock that she experienced it without me, but grateful that it gave her some peace during her menstrual. She was able to still live her life and be physically active when she desired.

On the first few days when you are only spotting, using a panty liner or a light pad is best. But when the flow comes IF you are mature enough to use tampons appropriately, they can make menstruating easier to bear in some instances.

Sleeping

When sleeping it is recommended to sleep with a dark towel under you or a cycle cloth of sorts. This will protect your bed from stains throughout the years. Locate a period tracker app on your mobile device to keep up with it. They will even notify you when you are getting closer to your expected period.

Free bleeding

Some women chose to bleed freely. They prefer to be out in nature and to let their cycle flow as it may. If they are inside, then they create soft plush seating for themselves with clean fresh towels that they carry around with them wherever they sit. When the day is done or when they feel the need, they refresh their bleed thrones and carry on. Surely it is a liberating experience that all women should experience one day. I am waiting for a time to try it. Meanwhile, organic is best.

Organic is best

Most pads and tampons are made from bleached cotton. It sounds as bad as it is. Many products are now becoming more mindful of the chemicals they may have used and created products made intentionally with organic cotton. There are organic pads as well as tampons available and even disposable underwear and reusable pads. Do your research and find what works best for you or your loved ones' flow.

I bleed on everything I love

There is a poem called, "The Period Poem." Written by Dominique Christina who performed it live in 2014. She was writing to a young man who was turned off by his girlfriend having a period. She mentions a line that says, "bleed on everything he loves." It happens, but more so we end up bleeding on everything we love. Especially if you have a partner or fellas if you have a mate. You are going to be exposed to her cycle and the bleeding she experiences. It's natural. Nothing for them to be ashamed of or for you to be afraid of.

Menstrual cups

This option came on the market about 15 years ago. It is called a menstrual cup. Made of soft plastic that is inserted into the vaginal canal and placed right outside of the cervix.

The cervix opening is where the lining of the uterus sheds during pregnancy and when pregnant, the place that must dilate to 10cm for the baby's head to emerge.

As a menstrual option, the cup can stay in place for up to 12 hours. During that time the cup will collect all the "period" that is released. This can range from 5ml- 80ml during the course of your period. Some lite days, some heavy. The average cycle is about 20 ml over the 3–7-day time frame. This could be about 5ml – 13ml per day. The collected menstrual cycle is nutrient-rich and can be easily flushed down the toilet, dried for a variety of uses, or poured in water to fertilize your garden. Researchers even found that menstrual catch could be used as regenerative medicine.

For measurement sake, keep in mind that it takes almost 30ml to equal an ounce. Ladies may feel like they are releasing multiple ounces of blood each day when it is much less. When removing it is important to gently squeeze the cup. Once removed you will finally be able to bask at the actual amount collected. The color can range from dark to bright red and may sometimes have clumps in it. Don't be alarmed. It's your body doing its job and cleaning up after itself when realizing you aren't pregnant this month.

CUAYing during Menstruation summary

There are certain birth control methods that stop or change your cycle. It is up to you and your health care provider to make the call of what is best for you. But if having a period is too painful or uncomfortable for you, you may want to start with creating monthly habits for yourself regarding your cycle. PMS: Proper Menstruation Seriousness. Be sure that you are eating balanced meals and drinking plenty of water the week prior to your cycle beginning. Leafy greens, healthy fats, fruits, and veggies, vitamins, and minerals. That is what your body is using to build the lining of your uterus and that is what your body will be releasing during your cycle. Respect it as a sacred time for you to go within and understand your body.

During your cycle, you will need to clean your genitals, and bathe more often. Shower, bath or sink wash-ups matter in keeping your vaginal area clean and fresh. Your hair and skin down below can hold odor, so you need to scrub it with gentle soap and warm water at least twice a day during your menstruation time of the month. I would love to go deeper into birth control and honoring your menstruation. But the goal here is for you to CUAY your way through. Hopefully, you found some tips here to make your cycle more enduring.

Intimate Hygiene (Reader discretion advised ages 14 and up or with parental guidance).

Sex is a beautiful thing. But it is not a game and should be taken extremely seriously because it is serious. In some cultures the act alone will bind you in marriage. Even though all we can see is the bodies intertwining, it is also everything that the other person has been exposed to that they bring to the table. It is a spiritual union as well. If you do not know the person, enough to know what they bring to the table spiritually you are opening yourself up to a world of the unknown. That is risky business. This part of our discussion in regard to CUAYing before and after Sex will start with the physical and end with more depth to what needs to be CUAYed after mingling sexually with another human.

Use the Bathroom

Before you engage in a sexual act it is understood that your body is in optimal health. You have no strange odors, bumps, or discharges and you have thoroughly CUAYed your genital area. It is also good to make sure that your bladder is empty before you interact.

After you finish a sexual encounter with your partner, there is always a tendency to just sit in it. Lay there staring off and replaying the experience in your mind. That is good to a point. Be sure that you are not drifting off to sleep or getting dressed and going on with your day, without using the bathroom and washing your body. It is not that the other person is dirty, but you do exchange intimate bacteria with them when your genitals intermingle. Even when using a condom, the base of the genitalia still caress, and bacteria is exchanged. Some ladies are sensitive to that and can easily develop a bacterial infection the first few times they engage with a new partner. So, wash soon after.

Front to back as a best practice translates to sex as well. Front area penetration should be happening before any back area penetration. This way you are sure that bacteria from the back door is not tracked into the front if you know what I mean.

Condoms Custody

Until you are in a committed relationship or marriage and ready to procreate ie. have children, it is vital that you use birth control. The easiest form of birth control for men to implement is using a condom. Once the sexual encounter is complete you/men should be the one removing and disposing of the semen. This means YOU keep the condom custody.

Inventive women have been known to use what was thought to be wasted and thrown in the trash to impregnate themselves. As a mother of a son, I recognize this is something that we should be educating our sons on. You can empty the semen, condom contents, into the toilet. Or tie the condom at the top and wrap it in tissue to dispose of later, if you are not at home. Another option is to catch and ingest.

Ingesting semen was likely NOT the CUAYing tip you came to read after sex, but there are nutrients in healthy semen that the male body releases, and ingesting it can add those back to your system. It is up to you to decide what is best for you. The goal is to protect your seed from unintended pregnancy. You can do this by being responsible for it every time it is released.

Conscious Release

There was a 36-year-old maid who impregnated herself with the used condom at the hotel where she worked. I'm sure she must have known he was a millionaire because she took him to court and won full child support benefits. There was another court case where the lady used the semen collected from a condom of a sex partner months later to impregnate herself and then took the man to court for child support. She took the sperm for IVF services and ended up with twins. She won and he had to pay. The judge said it was because "the semen was a gift." He gave it to her. It was an interesting case, and the truth is, if you release it, it is a gift.

Fellas be conscious of where you release your seed. Everybody is not deserving of it. For a man to have an orgasm* and release semen from his body, ejaculation is taxing to the body and equivalent to running 23 miles. That's twenty-three miles. Was it worth it? A partner has to be able to offer more than a nice and available body for you to exert 23 miles worth of energy and release vital nutrients that your body needs. Make sure the release is a conscious one. Choose wisely.

Men who ejaculate too often and overextend their bodies can overuse their prostate gland, which may lead to health issues later on. Don't waste your youth running 23 miles with partners that you won't even care about later. And then have your soul mate show up and your glands are too tired to perform. Learn to injaculate* and circulate it instead of releasing it. Or consider the ultimate hold back exercise, abstain until you're ready to claim a life partner. #YourWelcome

> "The genitals are not only used for reproduction they are organs of regeneration, organs of enlightenment, and organs of neuronal expansion."
> Dr. Jewel Pookrum, Straight from the Heart

Body and Hygiene Notes

_____

_____

_____

_____

_____

_____

_____

_____

> "Reflection or pondering must not be carried too far, lest either cripple the power of the decision. When the time for action has come, the moment must be seized."
>
> Wu Wei, I Ching Wisdom

CHAPTER SEVEN

―――

KEEPING A CLEAN HEART

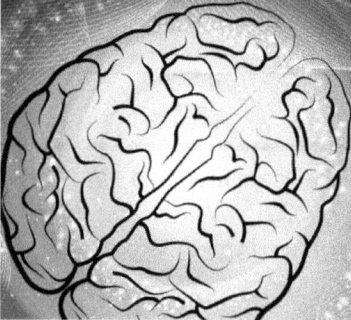

Chapter 7
Keeping a Clean Heart

Love is a beautiful thing when it works and even when it doesn't. Most people overall are good. They mean well. And then, there are snakes. It's up to you to sort them and know the difference. That's the first step in CUAYing through relationships. When you find that you are better off without someone or they walk away from you, it leaves a void. You have to find out how to fill it without spinning out of control, that's the balancing.

Purging

Before you can truly move on and let go of someone's presence in your life, you need to let go of the things you associate with them. Even if that means changing your routine, watching new shows, throwing out their gifts. Once you decide you are serious about moving on, there is no turning back. A true purge will sever the relationship.

If they come back and you try to work it out later, because you purged, it is hard for you to get the feeling you had before. The relationship is at ground zero. That person will have to woo you again. Is this partner the type who is consistent with their actions enough to put in the work again? Of course, there are surprises. When there are constant compatibility issues and not enough compromise you know a purge is approaching. Mind over matter wins every time. Like my sister always reminds me. Logic over feeling.

When I'm over someone, I don't even like the clothes that I had on taking pictures with them. They have to go too. Furniture, necklaces. Bye! Get your broom and sweep them out the door. Clean up after yourself from corner to corner. Don't worry, even tattoos can be removed or covered up. You'll get through the breakup. No matter if it was two weeks, 5 years, or a 25-year relationship, the purge is the first step towards CUAYing in newness.

"GOTTA GO"

If my ring tone could change based on the song I needed to hear at the moment. Today it would scroll to Bag Lady.

"Bag lady, you gon miss yo bus, dragging all these bags like that." Erykah Badu knew that we had to let go in order to find our way forward, and so did Monica. But Monica wasn't expecting to find me on the floor crying when she facetimed me that morning.

Monica was my sister... Well not really. We didn't share a parent by blood, but we'd shared so much life together since 15 that sisterhood seemed more accurate than a friend.

"Hey girl," I said as I answered. Knowing she was one of the people I couldn't hide from even if I tried.

"What's up boo?" What you doing on the floor in the closet? She said, noticing I was emotional.

"Nothing fits or it's dingy or not my style anymore!" I shouted through the tears.

"Girl, you crying over some clothes?" She said with a sarcastic tone.

"I guess so." I paused to prop my phone up on a pair of boots in the closet. "I mean I have a closet full of clothes and none of it really speaks to the woman I am now."

"Well throw it away," Monica said sternly.

"What you mean, I can't do that. I have to have something to wear." I spoke through the tears that wouldn't stop flowing.

"Listen, do you understand that you have been through a lot in the past year. You ended a ten-year marriage, moved three states away, and started a new life for your family. It makes sense that you don't want to keep dressing like the old you." She spoke authority.

Listening through the nose blowing I realized she was right. Most of my clothes were seasonal North Carolina gear anyway and Florida was pretty much summer and mild weather. Not so much cold. It was time, I had to let some things go.

Monica sat there with me that day. Sorting through the items of the past. Listening to the stories that I held surrounding certain items.

A few of the items I got from her. She was my hand-me-down friend and I loved vintage, so her old was sometimes my new and fly for me. I call it recycling. But even some of those were out-dated for me now.

"Look, this was my maternity dress from pregnancy," I told her thinking she'd see the vital reason to keep it. I twirled around in the distance. From her angle, she could only see my legs. But I could hear her laughing.

"Girl, your son is about to be 8, you can let that go now."

"No, that wasn't a dress from him, it was from when I was pregnant with Zenobia."

"Girl BYE!" "It's 12 years old and you ain't pregnant or about to be no time soon. Trash! Through that mess right on out. Gotta Go!" She said without a stutter.

"Well, my mama said don't through it away if someone else can use it." I had to slide that in there.

"Aye, donate it then. But I better not see your behind walking around here with no old maternity dress, A-GAIN!" Monica ended the conversation there.

But I laughed out loud so loud the children came in wondering what was going on. I asked Zenobia.

"What do you think of this dress?"

"It looks a little old, I mean, yeah. I've seen you wear that a lot." Zenobia replied as nicely as she could even though she was gently telling me I had been looking outdated and now was her opportunity to tell me.

"SEE," Monica said.

"Well dang, ya'll just going to gang up on me?"

"No, we trying to get you right for your new life."

All I could do was laugh. Thinking again about the look on her face when she realized I was holding on to a maternity dress from 12 years ago, that I thought I was rocking. When really it was cuter in memory than in actuality. I purged like never before that day.

My friend who was more like a sister to me in so many ways stood by me. She watched me bag up all my old things. Trash the rest and rearranged my new closet. It was clean and clear. She ushered me into a new mentality, holding me accountable for letting go of the old. I needed it.

I didn't have much. But what I had left, I liked. I held on to my favorite scarves, some nice solids for bottoms, and tops that I felt comfortable in. By the end of our facetime that day I was stronger. The tears were dried up and I was focused on moving forward.

Before we ended the conversation that evening Monica said, "you know what you should do? Bless your closet."

"What do you mean, bless my closet?"

"I mean this is what you have right now, but you have to see your walk-in closet and the home you want for your family now. That's what faith is." She completed her thought and went silent.

I let the silence set in. Took a deep breath and started blessing what I saw.

"Okay, well I am grateful for this closet. Everything that I kept remains for a reason. May everything here help me to feel more like my true self. May I walk knowing I'm beautiful and allow room for more to come. I give thanks in advance for my new walk-in closet that is coming my way. I know I deserve the best and I bless this closet and all those who get to meet me wearing all my stylist gear. And if I wake up tomorrow and don't have anything to wear, let Monica know it's her fault!" We both laughed... I laughed until I cried that time.

My heart was lighter though, so the tears weren't the same.

Filling the Void

After you purge and let go of things or people, you will need to begin to fill the voids. Whatever you do to fill the void of that person in your life, don't let it be destructive to your body. Excessive drugs or alcohol will not fill the void. Sexing the world and turning your body into community property will not fill the void. Not even binge-watching TV or any other mindless pleasures will fill the void. You have to find something constructive to do. My cousin Wise always said, "When the physical gets weak, build the mental." So rightfully so if the mind is weak, build the physical. Work out, garden, walk, run, ride, dance.

Dancing is an easy one because most people have some upbeat music that they like. No matter the genre. Play some tunes and move your body. It gets your heart rate up and can usually get you to smiling in no time. Don't play the songs you used to dance with them to or any love songs. Just move and be grateful they were removed to make room for who and what is meant for you. It may come tomorrow, next year, or in ten years, but the key is carrying joy while you are on the way. You can find all types of joy when you dance. Try it. Dance, shimmy, and shake.

Another option to fill in the void is to educate yourself on a topic of interest. Take up a trade, study yoga, or a foreign language. Start that blog you always wanted to create or that weekly workout club. Get your mind moving so it grows in the places that you used to overthink. Write a book, build a shed, create some art out of your situation. Music, painting, sculpt, learn to make waist beads or epoxy your coffee table. Just keep it moving... constructively.

You choose

As humans, we get a lot of creative freedom in our lives. We get to choose what we focus on and use our mighty words and human imaginations to see it prosper. Isaiah 55:11 says, *"My word, which comes from my mouth; it will not return to me void but will accomplish what I desire and achieve the purpose for which I sent it."* So, you decide. What kind of relationship do you want? Are you ready to reciprocate that? If not, it is totally okay to date and get to know people to find out what you want. Just be sure you are being honest with everyone and not creating any negative relationship karma for yourself along the way. You get what you give. Be gentle with people's hearts while you date.

Lesson review

No matter how amazing or bad the relationship was, there is always a lesson. Most of the time you don't have to look too far to find the lesson. It is usually in the red flags you ignored at the onset of the relationship. The nudges showing you the character you were trying to overlook. That's your lesson. But you didn't get the lesson until it was screaming at you or when they were screaming. There will be many lessons on the other side of an ended relationship. But be sure to take a close-up look at the character that you played and the role you took to get to that come. It takes two.

Physical detox

The thing that is the hardest to get over when moving on from love is the physical presence of the person. In this case, it is also beneficial to CUAY your body with a physical detox. There are so many options to choose from. You could go hard with the 7-day lemon water detox, the strict Daniel fast, or 21 days vegan, raw, juicing. There is also the herbal detox or the smooth move detox days. Research and commit to the one that works for you. Whatever you do, just let go of that "shit." Recycle it. Then forgive them and yourself for not being able to make it work. It happens.

Hydration

Dehydration is rampant around the world. Mostly by choice. Even with the freshest water available at all times, some people have a hard time actually doing it. Drinking water. Dehydrating our bodies is like draining our batteries and expecting them to power up fully. It won't. Your mind will slow down first, skin dries out, eyesight reduces, reflexes aren't as sharp and eventually, it begins to affect your organs. Their functionality diminishes over time with a lack of hydration. You are practically slowly killing yourself, in self-sabotage.

Create times in your day for intentional water breaks. Download an app on your phone to calculate your water consumption and send you reminders if needed. Hold yourself accountable. Try infusing your water with fresh herbs like basil or mint, lemon, lime, cucumber, ginger, pineapple, berries, or any other fruit or veggie you desire. Living up your water and increase your hydration by adding more fresh fruit to your diet. This will help to alkalize your body. Hydrated minds are happier, healthier, and more aware of potential snakes.

Keeping a Clean Heart Summary

So, you've hit the reset button on your relationship life. Congrats. Since then, you've purged, and filled in the voids. Your mind is determined, and you can clearly see what you want for yourself and what you don't want. The lessons are revealing themselves and you see how you contributed to the outcomes you have experienced. You've detoxed and paid better attention to your hydration. You have officially CUAYed that relationship. Next!

> *"Do the best you can until you know better.*
> *Then when you know better, do better."*
> *Dr. Maya Angelou*

A FAMILY THAT CUAY'S TOGETHER STAYS TOGETHER

CUAY

24/7

◄◄◄◄ /'KWAY'/

Clean Up After Yourself

CHAPTER EIGHT

THE CUAY CHALLENGE

Chapter 8
The CUAY Challenge

It all starts at home. Are you ready to CUAY before and after you meet a room? Are you ready to CUAY in the middle? Now is the time to take the CUAY Challenge when you are ready to, "Make CUAYing your lifestyle, and home a place you'd want to stay." It's easy, it's a poem. Memorize it for the best results.

Register with us for accountability and weekly surveys to collect CUAY data:

CUAY.org/cuay-challenge

Read the CUAY challenge then study the graphic organizers to follow. Week by week it will guide you through the expectations of infusing CUAYing into your lifestyle.

Over the 4 weeks, you will move from monitoring your home and actions in cleaning- to the full application of CUAYing in action.

CUAY CHALLENGE

What is CUAY you might say
It's moving with intention
can't stay in one place
When you CUAY You Clean Up After Yourself
Quick Slow and Thorough
Quickly get to the nearest sign of you
That jacket or bowl hairball or shoes
Just put it all where it goes
The rest is trash, for all you know
So give it a try before you leave that room,
Work for the day, or even that relationship you
finally left behind
Just get up and CUAY
Be Thorough, it's the way
Scan the scene
Slow to be sure it's **serene**
No sign of your path should be left in view
Now that you know CUAYing is what you do

S. DENISE KING

Wondering how to start the CUAY Challenge? It's easy.
Take it one day at a time, and set attainable goals. Complete the weekly checklist and pay attention to the focus areas.

GET READY TO

TAKE PICTURES
OF PROGRESS

SHARE THE CUAY
WAY

DEEP CLEAN
WEEKLY

CUAY

24 7

‹‹‹‹‹ /ˈKWAY/
Clean Up After Yourself

FOUR WEEK CHALLENGE
WEEKS 1 AND 2

**WEEK 1
FOCUS**

BEDROOM

25%
APPLICATION
75% MONITORING

WEEK 1 CHECKLIST

LEARNING THE 3
STEPS TO
CUAYING ✓

COMPLETE
1ST DEEP
CLEANING ✓

RE/NEW
BEDDING ✓

COMPLETE
YOUR WEEKLY
SURVEY ✓

CUAY.ORG

24 7

◀◀◀◀ /'KWAY'/
Clean Up After Yourself

WEEK 2 CHECKLIST

✓ SCRIBE THE
CUAY POEM
1-3 TIMES

✓ COMPLETE
2ND DEEP
CLEANING

✓ RE/NEW BATH
SOAP OR
TOWEL SET

✓ COMPLETE
YOUR WEEKLY
SURVEY

**WEEK 2
FOCUS**

**BEDROOM AND
BATHROOM**

50% APPLICATION
50% MONITORING

FOUR WEEK CHALLENGE
WEEKS 3 AND 4

WEEK 4 CHECKLIST

✓ TAKE SELFIES OR HOUSIES IN FAVORITE PLACE @HOME

✓ FINALIZE DEEP CLEANING FREQUENCY

✓ LEAVE A TESTIMONIAL ON CUAY.ORG & AMAZON

✓ COMPLETE YOUR WEEKLY SURVEY

WEEK 4 FOCUS

ENTIRE HOME EVERYWHERE

80% CUAYED HOME MOST OFTEN

CUAY.ORG

24 7

◀◀◀◀◀ /'KWAY'/

Clean Up After Yourself

WEEK 3 CHECKLIST

DOCUMENT AND DELEGATE HIGH RISK AREAS ✓

RE/NEW PLATES, SILVERWARE, POTS OR PANS ✓

COMPLETE 3RD DEEP CLEANING ✓

COMPLETE YOUR WEEKLY SURVEY ✓

WEEK 3 FOCUS

BEDROOM, BATHROOM, AND KITCHEN

75% APPLICATION AND 25% MONITORING

CHAPTER NINE

CUAYOLOGY

Chapter 9
CUAYology

CUAYology is the study of CUAYing and it is an art. It is using intuition plus common sense to overcome CUAYing hurdles and establishing order in your dome and home. The CUAY book intends to help keep families sane and homes maintained. As more and more people learn to CUAY their area and their history not only will there be happier families, but we will also create a happier world. There are levels of growth in CUAYing that can be linked to age or maturity. Below you will find the three stages of CUAYers, some scriptures to encourage your family's journey, and some final thoughts on cleaning up after yourself.

CUAY Starter

The CUAY starter is new to CUAYing. It is best to begin teaching toddlers to be CUAY starters. They need lots of modeling and teaching. You will show them how to do it and then over time allow them to do it alone. At the age of one or around the time they are walking they can begin to CUAY by putting their soiled diapers in the trash or into the diaper pail for reusable diaper wearers.

As you pay attention to the growth of your developing child you will be able to witness certain tasks that they can learn to become independent in Cleaning Up After Themselves. Next, they can learn to put the crayons up, or pick-up food particles that they dropped on the floor and collect for the trash. Each year they will add on to the CUAYing tasks they learned before. They are still learning the flow and finding the need to CUAYing. In general, this person is 1-7 years old.

We will also have some CUAY starters that are adults. Without being condescending, or making them feel small, you can still instruct them by modeling how to CUAY. Set some goals of things they can begin to be mindful of and hold them accountable for maintaining those things. Hopefully, they can move through this phase of being a CUAY starter in 1 year or less instead of 7. Uncleanliness is a hard habit to undo, so we want to give our adult CUAY starters time to practice and find consistency in their execution. During this time, you are modeling for them in some way various tasks that come across their path every day.

If you are a CUAY starter taking this journey alone. Congratulations. It takes courage to acknowledge you've been doing things wrong and take the initiative to change it. Take your time combing through the CUAY book and reminding yourself to CUAY All-Day and you can easily skip intern and move to the final CUAYing level.

If we are modeling cleaning for our children and allowing them to gain confidence in CUAYing various tasks, naturally around the age of 7, they are ready to move on in their CUAYing journey and take on more responsibility for cleaning themselves and their environment.

CUAY Intern

The CUAY intern emerges around the age of 7 through about 14. They have studied their parents or older siblings CUAY All-Day and are ready to take on full rooms and chores for themselves. We call them CUAY interns because they are familiar with the full process of CUAYing, however, they are not yet independent of maintaining a home or sometimes even their hygiene. It is important for parents to allow children to grow and mature in the CUAYing instead of stunting their development and enabling them to always be dependent on others to survive.

The CUAY intern is moving through tweenhood and puberty at this time and needs to learn about their bodies and how to CUAY them effectively. CUAY hygiene can be released to them at this time. The standard of CUAYing a home and body are not locked into their memory and they simply need repetition, accountability, and praise to stay the course. We all have days where the CUAY percentages of our home or hygiene fall short.

An older CUAY Intern needs that same reinforcement of repetition, accountability, and praise. Someone enabled them growing up. It doesn't matter who caused them to miss the CUAY lesson previously. We are teaching them now that they have to be responsible for themselves completely. Be sure to go through the CUAY deep cleaning guide and the CUAY body and hygiene thoroughly with them as a review. Highlight areas in your home that keep getting missed and work together to add them to your CUAY list.

If you are a CUAY Intern teaching yourself this method, you're almost there! You are one level away from being a CUAY Professional. But you have to master the Deep Cleaning and CUAY All-Day on the regular. You will have to hold yourself accountable to change from a lifestyle of "I'll get it later" to truly CUAYing through your daily activities.

CUAY Professional

The CUAY professional cleans by default at this point. It's ingrained in them. Remember even as children some people are naturally professionals in CUAYing regardless of their age. But by the time your child is 15 years old you need to be testing their CUAY All-Day skills and have little patience for them leaving a mess in their path. You only have 3 years left to solidify their ability to maintain the basics of a household and keep their body and hygiene in order.

Before your child journeys out into the world of college, workforce, or traveling the world, be confident that they know how to CUAY. The world will be looking at them as a reflection of your efforts. Make it count. Raise your children to be working towards being professional at cleaning. The goal is to CUAY around the globe with our families- to create communities and nations that CUAY All-day and strive to leave things better than they found them. Show the CUAY professionals in your life some appreciation for helping to maintain the household as a unit. With more than one pro in the home, it should be 80% or more maintained at all times.

Parents and loved ones, have you been teaching independence or dependence? We should be teaching in the direction the child should go. Trust that they can learn no matter where their developmental level is. As long as they are mobile, they can learn to CUAY in some way. You might be surprised to learn that they actually enjoy it or even better, that they prefer a CUAYed environment.

If you started off as a Cuay starter and now find yourself as a professional cleaner, thank you. I hope this text was able to articulate a standard path to keeping an orderly home! WOW. You truly responded with ability. Treat yourself to something special when you make it to a CUAY Professional after beginning as a starter or an intern. Have you found more order in your dome and home? Are you breathing deeper, appreciating your body on the regular, and finding CUAYing to be more of a lifestyle than a task now? That's the goal.

CUAYing is a journey of accountability and freedom with self. Thank you so much for taking the time to learn about CUAYing and sharing how easy the concept is with people you love.

When you move through the three stages of cuaying successfully, CUAY Starter, CUAY Intern to consistent CUAY Professional, you are a Certified CUAYologist. You are now charged with keeping your family sane and home maintained, even if you live alone!

> *"The mind, if bound with cords of lies, half truths, inferences, etc. cannot respond to truth even when it's being presented."*
> *Dr. Edward Robinson & Battle,*
> *Journey of the Songhai People*

CUAY Scriptures

Through the Bible and the teachings of the pattern man, Jesus (Yahshua, the son of God), there are so many amazing scriptures that we can quote and use to support our CUAYing journey. In this case, Jesus is referred to as *the pattern* because he came to life to show us how to live more abundantly and occupy our full power on earth through the word of The Beloved Creator. You may or may not follow the Bible or be familiar with the lessons therein, but be open-minded to the wisdom as it applies to the topic at hand. This is not a place for spiritual debate, but a place to acknowledge how these scriptures come alive in the way we interact with others and carry ourselves as humans. We are so blessed to have a pattern of the way so that we can seek guidance as needed.

The interpretations here are intentionally focused on bringing order by means of CUAYing. It is not intended to change anyone's religion only to offer guidance from a spiritual perspective. Of course, just like all interpretations, they can be seen in a variety of ways based on the reader. It is up to you to find the connections that make sense to you and apply them appropriately. Below you will find five scriptures that may help you understand the importance of CUAYing and establishing order in your dome and home.

Matthew 10:11-14

"Whatever town or village you enter, search there for some worthy person and stay at their house until you leave. As you enter the home, give it your greetings. If the home is deserving, let your peace rest on it; if it is not, let your peace return to you. If anyone will not welcome you or listen to your words, leave that home or town and shake the dust off your feet."

CUAY interpretation of this scripture:

As we travel and grow through life, we will stay in many different places. This scripture is important because it reminds you of your ultimate task. You must always look to offer peace wherever you go. In this case, our peace is to Clean Up After Yourself. Yes, we CUAY at home, but we are also charged with CUAYing publicly.

Yet, this message from the pattern man, teaches us that some places may not be worth your CUAYing effort. There is a line too far gone to bring it back to life. And some places where the people are not open to the greeting or "CUAY" that you bring. Do not waste your energy there. Use Matthew 10:11-14 to remind you to "let your peace return to you." Also, when you move on, do not carry it with you. Don't carry the worry of that situation or the time looking back over the details of the exchange. Simply, "shake the dust off your feet." This means, let it go and keep it moving. We have to do this in some relationships as well as some living situations.

Matthew 25:23

"Well done admirable one. You have been faithful over a few things, and I will make you the ruler over many things."

CUAY interpretation of this scripture:

What is being "faithful over a few things?" Well, at the root of that statement it has to mean taking care of the things you have. To take care of something you keep it well, clean, intact to the best of your ability. Be faithful over your bed, your room, bathroom, kitchen, etc. Be faithful over your body and your hygiene by keeping it clean, fresh and using quality products on your skin to limit the toxins that you ingest. When you are faithful over what you have it can be blessed. Maybe that means a bigger home or better neighborhood. It could mean healthier-looking skin and hair or a youthful glow that lasts through the years.

Establishing faithfulness over the few things that are under your control will open room for more to come into your life. Until you are faithful with what you have, you are not even deserving of receiving more. And in the event that you are blessed with more without being faithful, it typically shows.

The big house is a mess, the family is unhappy, or your bodily temple is obviously unkept.

To "rule over many things," you are conscious of the gift and in steady gratitude of what you have. Show your gratitude for life and yourself by being faithful with a few. Even if that means all you have is an air mattress on the floor in your grandma's basement. Make it home, an inviting space where love is felt. Bless it as you CUAY in the morning and when you rise every day. Put love in every corner. Be faithful with cleaning your sheets and maintaining order there. CUAY it all day and you will be "ruler over many" in time. Your territory will be increased.

2 Samuel 12:20

"Then David got up from the ground. After he had washed, put on lotions, and changed his clothes, he went into the house of the Lord and worshiped. Then he went to his own house, and at his request, they served him food, and he ate.

CUAY interpretation of this scripture:

If you are not familiar with the story of David, I'll leave that for your own backstory studying. To summarize, he was a worldly man who grew in his manhood after seeking God's own heart. He brought pain to others at some points in his life and experienced great pain towards him in his own journey. But later, he became a man of great praise! He danced. In 2 Samuel he was just faced with the death of his child. He was so low in spirit and in much pain. And then I think he decided to CUAY. But first, he had to get up from the ground. To get up signifies moving from a low place to a place of better. He had to move. He couldn't stay there if he wanted to feel a change. Once he was up, he washed himself.

To wash is a clear distinction of letting go of what was. He scrubbed the pain of his loss, but he didn't just stop there. Then he lotioned himself. Some people still don't see the use in moisturizing themselves. But David got up, washed, and lotioned himself before getting dressed. The getting dressed part mattered too. He could have just stayed naked or put-on tattered garments. But he dressed for what ended up being a feast. David hadn't eaten. He was fasting and questioning God, praying with everything he had for his child to live. But the child did not live.

Still, David knew if he wanted to live, he had to clean up after himself, maintain his hygiene and find the strength to move on. Food was his strength. And then he praised in the way he carried himself. He CUAYed through his pain. He worshipped anyway. You may be in a low place right now. Alone, misunderstood, trying to find peace. Take a few lessons from 2 Samuel. Get up and CUAY like David did.

Luke 11:34

"If thine eyes are clear the whole body will be full of light, but if it should be unclear, your body also shall be darkened."

CUAY interpretation of this scripture:

The eyes offer us sight in so many ways. Of course, it allows us to sense light and texture, faces and potholes too. But the eyes also speak to our focus. Even though we can have a wide peripheral view the focus can only be on one thing at a time. Whatever is in focus is clear or easily seen. Is your room clear, your kitchen sink, your toilet seat? Is your house in order? When's the last time you focused on your skin or looked at the ingredients of your lotion or soaps? What's your focus in life? What is clear to you right now?

CUAYing can help you answer all of those questions by getting your environment in order and it will allow you to see your path clearer. You can see what you need and what you don't need. You can see who is good for you and who is not. You can create space in your mind to imagine all the desires of your heart when your eye is clear. Dig deep to find out what you want and focus on that by CUAYing your way through and keeping distractions to a minimum.

Why do you keep tripping on that rug? Fix it or throw it away. Why are you still washing your hands in a cracked bowl? Replace it or fix your whole sink scenario so you don't have to keep maneuvering through life with broken pieces. Get clear about what you want so that your whole body can be full of light. The light is the guidance and the source of clarity.

Otherwise, the other half of Luke 11 is true as well. When the eye is unclear confusion looms. Things remain in the dark, so you are unable to see your way through. Too many moving parts with no cohesive direction. This may lead to a feeling of chasing your tail, pressing through life when your eye is not single and clear. Darkness prevails and you find yourself moving, but not going anyway. If you are ready to move, get clear. Focus on CUAYing to gain control of everything you can control. And leave the rest to the Master. The ultimate Source. CUAY until your way is clear.

Psalm 119:18

"Open my eyes that I may see, the wonderful things in your law."

<u>CUAY interpretation of this scripture:</u>

The last scripture to be shared on this topic is from Psalm 119:18. This one is short but powerful. To open your eyes is to change from a sense of darkness to a sense of clarity. To ask for your eyes to be open is to acknowledge that there can be some things that you are missing that you want to have the wisdom to view with clarity. But we just don't want to see any and everything. That would be too much for us to process. We need to focus on seeing the wonderful things in the Most Highs law.

If you are focusing on the negative, then you will see more of that in your life. If you are focusing on the wonderful things you will too, see more of that in your life. The beauty is in us having a choice on what we want to focus on. To ask the all-knowing to open our eyes is to humbly say, "I can't see without you." There are so many wonderful things to behold. But when our lives and minds are cluttered, we miss the wonderful because we are so bogged down in the mess. Ask for eyes to see the wonder, eyes to focus on the beauty, and watch those things show up more and more in your life.

If you know of other scriptures or spiritual texts that relate to CUAYing share them @CUAYlife.

Closing

Creating a CUAYing mind is one that understands we make an imprint on the world daily in how we engage with life. Do you wake up and mess up your surroundings? Are you creating a storm path wherever you go? Does your body get the CUAYing attention it requires daily? Are your crevices clean? If you have followed the CUAYing journey you've found some tips and tools to help establish more peace in your life at home, as well as mentally. Remember, a family that CUAY's together makes room for shared responsibility. Any task alone is harder, but when we each contribute, we ease the load. This goes for maintaining a house and growing stronger relationships with those in our lives.

We've walked through this content Quick, Slow, and Thorough and it is time for the full application. Information is nothing without application. In closing, it is vital to reiterate that cleaning up after yourself is a journey of self that impacts the whole. When we raise our children or ourselves, the least we can do as collective humans is to teach them to CUAY. Creating a society where people CUAY on purpose for themselves and others can help to soften our exchange as a people. It will lighten the load of those who can become exhausted with CUAYing for everyone, and it can empower those who never CUAYed to find the beauty in the independence that CUAYing offers.

This is a lifestyle, a standard of living that was intended to help families grow closer and for individuals to understand the motion of themselves a little deeper. This is not a religious text; however, it is rooted in the word of God as mentioned in the chapter above and knowing "cleanliness is so next to Godliness." Mastering both can positively impact the human experience in a magnificent way. This is timely wisdom passed down through generations and evolved into the CUAYing needs of our time.

So, did you take the CUAY challenge? I look forward to hearing all the CUAY stories and seeing the before and after images of how CUAYing impacted your dome and home. Please share @CUAYlife on social media. Check out our CUAY reminders and support this movement with some gear for you or a gift for a loved one at CUAY.org. Let's share this mission with those in need. It has been a pleasure to unpack these lessons with you. I pray they are understood and useful in you establishing order in your dome and home.

Be well.

Mother, Lover, Publicist, Birth Assistant, Earth Ambassador

S. Denise King, MPA CUAYologist

CUAY Reminders
CLEAN UP AFTER YOURSELF
Welcome to Cuayville
CUAY
/'KWAY'/
CUAY.ORG

Quick CUAY Reminders

CUAY Reminders

CLEAN UP AFTER YOURSELF

CUAY©
Starter
/'KWAY'/
Clean Up After Yourself

cradle to
gradeschool

MAKE A STATEMENT

Teach yourself to

CUAY©

◄◄◄◄ /'KWAY'/

Clean **U**p **A**fter **Y**ourself

If your socks are dirty, so is your floor!

CUAY FLOORS DAILY

C U A Y
/'KWAY/
CLEAN UP AFTER YOU

CUAY©

All-Day

/'KWAY'/

Clean **Up** After **Y**ourself

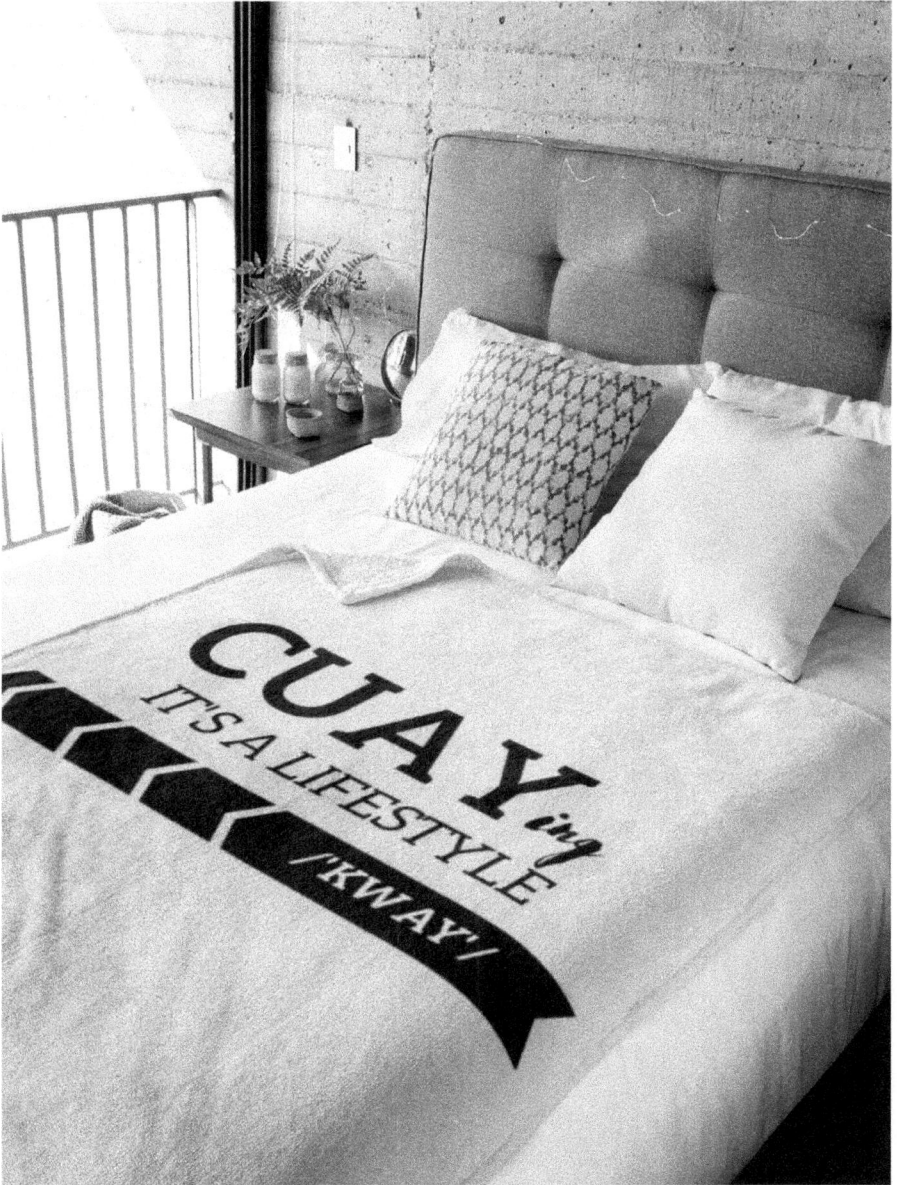

NOW I CUAY ME DOWN TO SLEEP

CUAY

24/7

/'KWAY'/

Clean Up After Yourself

MAMA TAUGHT ME TO CUAY

CUAY

24/7

◄◄◄◄◄ /'KWAY'/

Clean Up After Yourself

He Cuays like his Daddy

CUAY

24/7

◀◀◀◀◀ /'KWAY/

Clean Up After Yourself

NOT NEW TO THIS

Cuaying
Since 1981

CUAY

24/7

/'KWAY'/

Clean Up After Yourself

Graphic gear and quotes of CUAY
Reminders are available for purchase or
custom request at
CUAY.org

Support the CUAY movement.

#CUAYaroundTheWORLD
#CUAYlife
#CleanUpAfterYourself
#AdoptaWord
#CUAY

Stay tuned for our glossary...

Glossary

We have come to the end of our CUAYing journey and now look to dive a little deeper into the text. Just in case you need further explanation or for a deeper understanding of the content, the CUAY glossary can be useful. Below you will find 50 words that may be new to you or you may need the author's perspective on those words to gather the intended meaning.

Words listed in alphabetical order.

1.   **activated charcoal:** a fine black powder made from bone char, coconut shells, peat, petroleum coke, coal, olive pits, or sawdust that is activated by being processed at very high temperatures and when ingested can be used to absorb toxins and chemicals from the body. It is not to be confused with charcoal briquettes used for grilling, which are toxic to the body if ingested and processed differently than activated charcoal.

2.   **antioxidants:** substances such as vitamins C and E, selenium, and carotenoids, such as beta-carotene, lycopene. They protect your cells against free radicals that lead to heart disease, cancer, and other diseases.

3.   **baking soda:** also known as sodium bicarbonate is a simple chemical compound, found in crystalline form in nature but is ground to a fine powder for use in cooking, home, and health care. It comes out of the ground in the form of minerals or from evaporated lake basins.

4.   **beingness:** at the moment of birth, you ARE. You are present and alive. That is the basic state of being. As you mature that beingness is the quiet-natural you without labels or status. Just you.

5.   **chafing:** skin rubbing against itself causing inflammation and an open wound on the surface of the skin. Can lead to infection if not managed appropriately.

6.   **circumcision:** a medically unnecessary surgery and a socially accepted act of amputating four parts of the upper foreskin of the male penis. Typically done at birth or puberty, originally said to be a religious act, now done as a cultural tradition in various places around the world.

7.   **clitoridectomy:** a medically unnecessary surgery done on female genitals where the clitoris is removed. The intention is to reduce female sexual appetite before marriage. One type of female circumcision.

8.   **clitoris:** the pleasure center of the female reproductive glands located at the top under the vulva and clitoris hood. It appears to be a small often coin-sized organ above the surface but is mostly buried inside the reproductive system of the female. Three-fourths of the clitoris is below the surface of the skin. When active it stimulates hormones and activates a type of orgasm in women.

9.   **crevices:** areas in a home or on a body that can be often over-looked when cleaning. Checking the crevices will tell you if that area is as clean as you think.

10.   **dartos muscle:** a part of the male reproductive organ, the dartos is a smooth muscle that lies just below the skin and acts to regulate the temperature of the scrotum. In the shaft, this muscle is used to protect the head of the penis from damage or scarring. It is one of the four parts of the gland commonly removed during circumcision.

11.   **ejaculation:** commonly the peak of a male orgasm when semen is released from the reproductive tract. When in the presence of a female egg, pregnancy may occur.

12.   **eliminate:** to eliminate is to remove from current position. Part of CUAYing is sorting and one pile that you will have to keep in rotation is the trash pile. This is where you eliminate the things you no longer need.

13.   **equinox:** two points of the year when the day and nights are equal. Fall and Spring equinoxes are times of the year to bring your life into balance and hit the reset button your home and body deep cleaning.

14.   **excision:** One type of female circumcision where the skin is cut away from the sex organ. In this case, the vulva is removed from the female body.

15.   **exfoliate:** to gently cleanse the outer layer of the surface or skin and can stimulate new skin cells to grow. This typically leads to clearer skin and smaller visible pores. On teeth, exfoliation helps eliminate tartar build-up.

16.   **foreskin:** a natural covering of the penis at birth. It serves to keep the head of the penis protected and during intercourse assists in keeping the partners' vaginal canal moist, as the cut penis pulls moisture out during the engagement. #ForeskinFan

17.   **Frankincense:** resin from the Boswellia tree found in India, Africa, and the Middle East commonly rolled into incense. Traditionally used in mummification and burned during spiritual practices, meditation, and prayer. #Cleaning

18.   **frenulum:** a small ridge or folded area located on the penis below the head and at the base of the foreskin. It is used to retract the foreskin of an intact penis. One of the four parts of the penis is removed during circumcision.

19.   **grooming:** typically used to describe the care of pets, however, grooming can be used to communicate the intentional care of the human body as well.

20.   **high fructose corn syrup:** a highly used chemically processed corn syrup found in most processed foods on shelves. More recent research has found it can be harmful to the human body over time and should be reduced or eliminated from most diets. Check labels for other names that this chemical may be hidden under.

21.   **hygiene:** the process of maintaining the wellness of the body through thorough care and cleaning.

22.   **infibulation:** narrowing the vaginal opening after circumcision by stitching the female genitalia together. This is another time of female circumcision that is still legal and happening in 28 countries to date.

23.   **infused:** to mix or merge things.

24.   **injaculation:** or injaculate, a well-hidden art of men withholding their semen during an orgasm, or semen retention. It is used in tantric practices to sustain the male's energy and keep him from over-using his reproductive organs and depleting his life force. It's very beneficial in extending the sexual encounter and allowing partners to achieve multiple orgasms.

25.   **karma:** the experience of time giving you back what you gave out. Karma can be a friend or an enemy based on your current actions and the seeds you plant today. Every action has a reaction.

26.   **labia:** the external folds of the vulva that drape the clitoris and enclose the vaginal opening.

27.   **longevity:** the intention to live a long life and add to it by caring for yourself sufficiently daily.

28.   **minerals:** naturally occurring elements in the earth and whole foods that our bodies need to grow and function normally.

29.   **MSG:** Mono-Sodium-Glutamate is a common food additive that is known to increase appetite. Its usage has increased over time and many people are now developing adverse effects and allergies from ingesting it.

30.   **Nutrient-rich:** substances or foods that naturally carry large amounts of nutrients that the human body needs.

31.   **orgasm:** the peak of a sexually exciting experience when hormones create a feeling of bliss that circulates the entire body. It is a sacred time of love that can be used to pray or create when combined with a compatible partner or in solo-cultivation.

32.   **penis:** the rod of the male reproductive system that is used to engage in sexual encounters or eliminate liquid waste.

33.   **postpartum depression:** a type of depression that can be activated after birth for some women. Without proper help and support, it can last months or years.

34.   **purge:** to rapidly release things that no longer serve you. Ranging from clothes, food stored, acquaintances, or a state of mind.

35.   **ridged band:** wrinkly skin inside the foreskin tip. It contains loads of nerve endings that help to increase pleasure during sexual encounters. One of the four parts of the penis is removed during circumcision.

36.   **ROY-G-BIV:** an acronym to remember the color lineup of the rainbow. Red, orange, yellow, green, blue, indigo, violet. Can be used to organize spaces with various colors. Closets, collectibles, etc.

37.   **sage:** a traditional herb dried and used to purify the air.

38.   **scrotum:** smooth muscular skin sack used to house the testes of the male reproductive system.

39.   **Sea Moss:** a popular super seafood used to make a gel. Has been found to contain 92 of the minerals that the body needs daily.

40.   **serene:** peaceful, relaxing, not disrupted or overstimulating.

41.   **shimmy:** an internal vibration that makes it way to the surface of your body and all your muscles start to move with intention. It is a strong movement right before a shake that can happen over the entire body. #ShimmyTime

42.   **solstice:** two points of the year when the seasons are in transition and the days out way the nights (Summer Solstice), or the night out ways the day (Winter Solstice).

43.   **systemically:** a vital part of the whole, that if affected negatively can harm the whole system.

44.   **teach:** to offer information to students who are open to learning, in a way that they can receive and develop from it. Students may also locate information to teach themselves. Always note that teachers are lifelong students in some way.

45.   **technique:** a strategic way of doing things that helps to reach the goal most effectively. Ongoing practice will allow for a technique to be developed.

46.   **testes:** vital organs in the male reproductive system that house immature spermatozoa that are later released to mature for reproduction.

47. **thorough:** finishing to competition intentionally. Not doing anything halfway, but fully to the best of your ability. #BeThorough

48. **Unrefined Virgin Coconut Oil:** the oil from coconuts that has not been heated or processed and actually still smells like the coconut. Another multiuse food supplement.

49. **Vagina:** also known as yoni, is a canal housed in the female reproductive system. It is a portal from heaven for babies making their way to earth and also offers a glimpse to a heavenly experience for partners who are welcomed during intimate encounters.

50. **Wellness:** a state of balance in mental, emotional, physical and spiritual health where the being is able to experience overall peace.

INQUIRE MORE:

_____

_____

_____

_____

_____

_____

_____

_____

| *Inquire until you're inspired.* |

www.ingramcontent.com/pod-product-compliance
Lightning Source LLC
Chambersburg PA
CBHW070033100426
42740CB00013B/2673